NAVY

AND

MARINE CORPS

PERFORMANCE

WRITING

GUIDE

3RD EDITION
www.servicebooks.com

NAVY AND MARINE CORPS PERFORMNCE WRITING GUIDE

Published by: Professional Management Spectrum, Inc.

PO Box 30330
Pensacola, Florida 32503
Phone: (800) 346-6114

Web: www.servicebooks.com

ISBN: 0-9623673-7-0

PRINTED IN THE UNITED STATES OF AMERICA

TABLE OF CONTENTS

PERSONAL AWARDS & INDIVIDUAL RECCOGNITION

PERFORMANCE APPRAISALS

FAVORABLE

UNFAVORABLE

PERFORMANCE DICTIONARY

PERSONAL AWARDS

AND

INDIVIDUAL RECOGNITION

PERSONAL AWARDS AND INDIVIDUAL RECOGNITION

In this section, PERSONAL AWARDS includes Navy Commendation Medals, Navy Achievement Medals, and other individual award medals. INDIVIDUAL RECOGNITION includes Letters of Commendation and Letters of Appreciation.

The degree of accomplishment or achievement demonstrated by an individual, including under what conditions or circumstances, dictates which award or recognition might be appropriate for individual performance. The Navy and Marine Corps Awards Manual set forth individual award criteria. Guidelines for earning Letters of Commendation and Letters of Appreciation are issued by local commanders.

This section does not attempt to categorize performance into a particular award area or level. This section was developed to provide guidance on how to draft personal award and individual recognition documents once a particular level of performance has been identified.

Drafting a Letter of Appreciation is a one-document, one-step process. A variety of example Letters of Appreciation are provided later in this section.

The drafting of personal awards and most Letters of Commendation is a two-document process. A CITATION and a SUMMARY OF ACTION draft are required.

The following guidance is offered for these two distinctly different drafts.

PERSONAL AWARDS

CITATION

The CITATION must meet strict, rigid requirements of uniformity and consistency.

NAME HEADING

Type complete name and rank/rate in capitol letters. Although the exact number of lines used to list this information is not mandated at the Department of the Navy level, the information is routinely displayed in three lines for enlisted members and two lines for officers.

ENLISTED HEADING EXAMPLES

INFORMATION SYSTEMS TECHNICIAN
JOHN JAMES KENNEDY
UNITED STATES NAVY

CHIEF YEOMAN (SUBMARINES)
JOHN JAMES KENNEDY
UNITED STATES NAVY

SERGEANT
JOHN JAMES KENNEDY
UNITED STATES MARINE CORPS

OFFICER HEADING EXAMPLES

LIEUTENANT (JUNIOR GRADE) JOHN JAMES KENNEDY, III
UNITED STATES NAVY RESERVE

LIEUTENANT COMMANDER JOHN JAMES KENNEDY, JR
UNITED STATES NAVY

MAJOR JOHN JAMES KENNEDY
UNITED STATES MARINE CORPS

CITATION NARRATIVE

GENERAL RULES:

1. DO NOT USE – "YOU" (Write in THIRE PERSON, i.e. HE, SHE.)

2. DO NOT USE – Names, terms, etc. that are not readily and easily understandable to people not in the military.

3. DO NOT USE – "Petty Officer Second Class Kennedy" (use "Petty Officer Kennedy.")

4. DO NOT USE – Abbreviations such at LT, SN, etc, (Use Lieutenant, Seaman, etc.)

5. DO NOT USE – Information not included in the Summary of Action.

6. Local directives usually dictate the maximum number of typewritten lines allowed in the narrative. The general range is 15-20 lines. Check local reference material to assure conformance.

CITATION NARRATIVE PARTS

The citation narrative can be broken down into three distinct parts with specific information required in each part.

PART ONE

Part ONE gives standard wording for a particular award, the job/billet held, the command (and location if applicable), and the inclusive period of the award. The Navy and Marine Corps Awards Manual provides specific wording which is to be used for each award. As an example, the Navy Achievement Medal may be awarded for either PROFESSIONAL ACHIEVEMENT or LEADERSHIP ACHIEVEMENT. All Navy Achievement Medals awarded for PROFESSIONAL ACHIEVEMENT require the wording" "For professional achievement in the superior performance of his duties…"

EXAMPLE:
"For professional achievement in the superior performance of his duties while assigned to (job/billet), (division, department, branch, etc.), (command), from (starting date) to (ending date.)"

"For professional achievement in the superior performance of his duties while serving (in/in the) (organization) on board (command) (during Indian Ocean operations), from (starting date) to (ending date.)"

PART TWO

Part TWO starts with a single sentence which identifies the recipient by name and lists the outstanding personal attributes displayed. Following this first sentence note the highlights of his or her actual accomplishment and/or performance. The amount of space (total typewritten lines) available normally limits this information to three or four sentences.

PART TWO – FIRST SENTENCE EXAMPLES

…Displaying consistently high qualities of technical skill, resourcefulness, and dedication in the execution of his duties, (Name) demonstrated exceptional performance in a position of great responsibility.

…Displaying consistently exceptional qualities of mature judgment, loyalty, integrity, and meticulous attention of detail in the execution of his duties, (Name) displayed exceptional performance in a position of added responsibility.

…(Name) consistently displayed exceptional competence, sound judgment, and depth of professional knowledge in the execution of his responsibilities.

…Displaying outstanding skill and resourcefulness, (Name) contributed directly to …

5

…Displaying consistently exceptional qualities of leadership and management skill, (Name) demonstrated superior performance in a position of added responsibility.

…(Name) consistently performed his demanding duties in an exemplary and highly professional manner.

…(Name) displayed an exceptional degree of personal initiative in …

..(Name), through his outstanding professional knowledge, enthusiasm, and devotion to duty, contributed significantly to …

…(Name), through foresight, outstanding technical knowledge, and exemplary watch standing ability played a vital role in …

…(Name) consistently performed her demanding duties in an exemplary and highly professional manner.

…(Name) demonstrated exceptional leadership and managerial skills and performed her duties in an exemplary manner.

(Name) outstanding leadership and technical competence resulted in …

…(Name) inspirational leadership and enthusiastic dedication to duty resulted in …

…(Name) exceptional personal involvement and dedication to duty resulted in …

…(Name) consistently executed his responsibilities in an exemplary and highly professional manner.

…(Name) initiative, meticulous attention to detail, and professionalism was instrumental in …

…The professional dedication and devotion to duty exhibited by (Name) resulted in …

...(Name) distinguished himself by performing his duties in an exemplary and highly professional manner.

...(Name) aggressively responded to significantly increased responsibilities with enthusiasm and uncommon dedication.

(Name) professionalism and impeccable leadership contributed to the highly successful ...

...(Name) consistently performed her demanding duties in an exemplary and highly professional manner, which greatly contributed to ...

...During this period, (Name) enthusiastic leadership, outstanding managerial ability, and keen judgment were major factors in the highly successful ...

...(Name), through foresight, outstanding technical knowledge, and exemplary watch standing ability, played a vital role in the successful ...

...Displaying exceptional skill, leadership and technical expertise, (Name) was directly responsible for significant improvement in ...

CITATIN PART TWO - AFTER THE FIRST SENTENCE

...Her professional advice on technical matters and her ability to elicit maximum effort from those around her earned the respect and admiration of the officers with whom she worked.

...His superb ability to develop and execute large, complex managerial undertakings increased the (...) capabilities of the command. He earned the respect of all officers and men with whom he was associated by exhibiting outstanding professional knowledge while maintaining an acute sensitivity to the needs of his men and the command.

…Without formal training he expertly documented a voluminous number of (…). Voluntarily working exceedingly long hours, he was singularly responsible for (…).

…He developed new (…) control procedures within the command which resulted in more efficient management of (…). The procedure significantly contributed to the upgrade of (…) and increased mission effectiveness.

…His perseverance and total dedication ensured a (…) program which exceeded all expectations and requirements. He was instrumental in developing a new (…) system that had an immediate and positive impact on mission readiness and will continue to be highly beneficial in the years to come.

…His professional accomplishments and established training objectives will have a continued impact on future training and operations throughout the (organization).

…He planned and directed implementation of the (…) program, managed (…), and personally devised an ingenious (…) plan. His diligent efforts and unending resourcefulness inspired all who observed him and contributed significantly to the mission of the command.

…His sustained initiative and drive in generating new ideas and approaches in resolving (…) difficulties achieved a marked increase in the reliability of (…).

PART THREE

Part THREE ends the citation by naming the recipient and listing the personal attributes mentioned or implied in PART TWO, followed by "reflect great credit upon himself and was/were in keeping with the highest traditions of the United States Naval Service." For Marines, the citation ends with: "…reflected great credit upon himself, the United States Marine Corps and the United States Naval Service."

EXAMPLES

...(Name) exceptional professional ability, initiative and loyal dedication to duty reflect great credit upon himself and the United States Naval Service.

...(Name) unsurpassed loyalty and professionalism reflected great credit upon himself and were in keeping with the highest traditions of the United States Naval Service.

...(Name) initiative and devotion to duty were in keeping with the highest traditions of the United States Naval Service.

...(Name) loyalty, dedication to duty, and outstanding performance throughout reflected great credit upon himself and the United States Naval Service.

...(Name) exceptional professional ability, self-motivation, initiative, and loyal dedication to duty reflected great credit upon himself and were in keeping with the highest traditions of the United States Naval Service.

...(Name) dedication and loyal devotion to duty reflected great credit upon himself and are in keeping with the highest traditions of the United States Naval Service.

...(Name) performance reflected great credit upon himself and was in keeping with the highest traditions of the United States Naval Service.

...(Name) extraordinary professionalism, initiative, and loyal dedication to duty reflected great credit upon himself and were in keeping with the highest traditions of the United States Naval Service.

...(Name) leadership, initiative, and selfless devotion to duty reflected great credit upon himself and were in keeping with the highest traditions of the United States Marine Corps and the United States Naval Service.

SUMMARY OF ACTION

The Summary of Action is what reviewing/approving authorities scrutinize closely to determine if approval of an award is justified based on the criteria set forth in the Navy and Marine Corps Awards Manual.

Before attempting to write the Summary of Action, the drafter should know exactly all requirements stipulated for the award. For example, to be eligible for a Navy Achievement Medal for "professional achievement," the Award Manual states that an individual must:

    "(a) clearly exceed that which is normally required or expected, considering the individual's grade or rate, training, and experience, and

    "(b) be an important contribution which is of benefit to the United States and the Naval Service."

The Summary of Action MUST contain sufficient information to overpoweringly convince reviewing/awarding authorities that the individual being recommended for the award is fully deserving. This section MUST contain specific, and where appropriate, quantifiable, information (i.e. saved the Navy $30,000; reduced manpower requirements by 30,000 man-hours, etc.).

There is no minimum or maximum length to the Summary of Action, so long as sufficient evidence is presented to justify approval of the award. Three pages of "glittering" generalities (i.e. top performer, limitless potential, etc.) will not carry as much convincing evidence as a single page of well documented "facts" on what was accomplished and how the individual directly contributed to the accomplishment.

After all pertinent, specific efforts and actions are committed to print, the results of the actions must fully meet the criteria for the award as set forth in the Awards Manual. For example, in the case of a Navy Achievement Medal, the performance must: "Be an important contribution which is of benefit to the United States and the Naval Service."

If the Summary of Action does not fully support this requirement, there is no valid reason to approve (or recommend approval) of the award.

SUMMARY OF ACTION – EXAMPLE #1

(Name) displayed outstanding professional performance from (starting date) to (ending date) while serving on (organization). During this period he made valuable and lasting contributions to command operational readiness and effectiveness. In his first assignment as (...) he was faced with developing and implementing a training program that would prepare an inexperienced crew of (number) personnel for full-scale operations. He launched himself into his new and unaccustomed duties with uncommon zeal and vitality, working almost around the clock developing (...) standards for virtually every supervisory and operational position in (organization). Within (...) months qualifications were established and specific individual objectives were mandated. The program was such a success that in the next (...) months (organization) received (number) performance evaluations with a grade of "OUTSTANDING" by (organization). His (...) program enjoyed similar success. Overall qualification increased dramatically from (...) to (...) percent in less than (...) months. As a final measure of his comprehensive training effort, (number) out of (number) were advanced during his tenure in this demanding billet.

During (...) operations (Name) was cited in official correspondence by (organization) and (organization) for his professionalism and sterling performance.

As manning decreased significantly during (...) period, (Name) volunteered for more responsibilities, including those of (...) and (...). Within a short time he had assumed no fewer than (number) of primary and collateral duties, more than any other person in (organization). Each area of responsibility received his full attention and he labored long hours before and after the normal work day ensuring that all tasks and projects were

11

completed on or ahead of schedule. His assignment to (...) duties proved immensely successful, (number) of (number) accomplished (...).

(Name) mastery of any and all assignments ultimately led to his selection to one of the most demanding billets at (organization). As (billet title) he was tasked with the enormous duty of (...) and he proved more than equal to the challenge. As a direct result of his diligent, untiring efforts, (organization) accomplished (...).

(Name) professional performance, initiative, and devotion to duty throughout his tour cannot be adequately reflected in a performance appraisal and is unquestionably worthy of recognition of this special award.

SUMMARY OF ACTION – EXAMPLE #2

For professional achievement in the superior performance of his duties while serving as (billet) on (organization) from (starting date) to (ending date). Throughout this period (Name) displayed consistently exceptional qualities of managerial skill, loyalty, leadership, and meticulous attention to detail in the execution of his duties.

(Name) foresaw well in advance the need for an orderly transition of (organization) into a new operational environment. In a superbly well organized and executed multi-phase plan, he first committed organization structure and responsibility to print, followed up with discussions broken down into appropriate pay grades, and then trained and assigned virtually every manager and supervisor in the implementation of their particular area of responsibility. Throughout this period immediate objectives and long range goals were established and effectively managed through comprehensive, yet simple to administer, procedures that he devised and tracked. Through extensive personal knowledge and planning (organization) structure was completely revamped and ready for operations in less than (...) percent of the anticipated time, and at a savings of (...) man-hours and (...) dollars.

The single document and the follow-up personal leadership set the operational and management framework that initially drove the (organization) early organization and efforts. As (organization) manning started to increase to full allowance he announced, discussed, and then implemented expected professional and leadership standards throughout the ranks. In addition, he personally assisted virtually every supervisor in military and technical areas of responsibility, including (…).

(Organization) subsequently passed a variety of operational and administrative inspections, including (…) and (…). Of equal significance, during this entire evolution (organization) morale remained high and reenlistment and advancement records reached an amazing (…) percent.

Throughout this period, (Name) sterling performance of duty and total contribution to the mission and improvement of (organization) was indeed beyond the normal call to duty. The imprint of his managerial skills, leadership, devotion to duty, and exemplary performance will have a continued impact on future (organization) operations and mission accomplishment.

INDIVIDUAL RECOGNITION

Individual recognition, excluding Personal Awards discussed earlier, consists of Letters of Commendation and Letters of Appreciation.

Letters of Commendation may or may not contain a CITATION and a SUMMARY OF ACTION. If both are required, follow the Personal Awards procedures and examples. If letter form only is used, see the information on the following pages and replace APPRECIATION with COMMENDATION where appropriate.

Most commands encourage maximum use of Letters of Appreciation (LOAs) to recognize deserving personnel. LOAs are relatively easy to write and they do not require excessive research or documentation. Remember, commanding officers are not the only ones who can issue LOAs. Almost any senior can give a subordinate due recognition through a LOA. However, the more noteworthy the performance or accomplishment, the higher the LOA should go for signature.

People appreciate being officially recognized for superior performance. Additionally, timely recognition for quality performance gives the person receiving the LOA and others around him or her additional incentive and motivation. LOAs are an effective tool for improving performance and morale throughout an organization. Commanding officers are fully aware of the relationship between positive, timely and official recognition, and improved overall performance. Therein lies a personal benefit for the superior who drafts LOAs for deserving subordinates.

By writing LOAs for deserving personnel, the superior has demonstrated to his commanding officer that he or she knows how to use effective leadership principles. Maximum use of LOAs should be a fundamental part of any organization.

LETTERS OF APPRECIATION

Letters of Appreciation usually encompass three primary areas:

    (1) The event/activity, and date involved:

    (2) A listing or notation of personal accomplishments or achievements along with the personality traits displayed; and,

    (3) Appropriate closing "thank you" remarks>

In general, a Letter of Appreciation (or Commendation) has three numbered paragraphs, one covering each of the above areas.

The examples on the following pages are provided to show the kind or type of material that might be used in each paragraph.

LOA – EXAMPLE # 1

From:

To:

Subj: LETTER OF APPRECIATION

1. I take great pleasure in expressing my appreciation for your outstanding performance while assigned as/to (job) during the period (date) to (date).

2. Your duties included (list duties). Throughout this time frame you executed your duties in an exemplary manner. You were quick to offer suggestions and viable ideas for improvement of (...). Several of your ideas have been implemented and have enhanced (area). You are a very reliable individual who consistently produced superior results. Your ever present considerate attitude and congenial disposition were positive assets in your day-to-day dealings with others. Your military appearance and bearing continually reflected your obvious pride in your work and the Naval Service. You approached problem situations intelligently and methodically, always employing the best use of resources at hand in their resolution.

3. Your keen sense of responsibility in the performance of your duties reflects great credit upon yourself, and is in keeping with the highest traditions of the United States (Navy or Marine Corps). WELL DONE.

/Signature/

LOA – EXAMPLE # 2

From:
To:
Subj: LETTER OF APPRECIATION

1. During the period (date) to (date) you were assigned to the (element) of (organization). You performed your duties as (job) in an outstanding manner and helped contribute directly to the overall mission accomplishment of the command. Your dedication to duty and constant insistence on error free performance was instrumental in (organization) earning the following distinctions (list). Your outstanding efforts, in all areas of responsibility, have resulted in an overall upgrade of (area).

2. Your (number) years of (Navy/Marine Corps) service included assignments to (list). Your devotion to duty and outstanding support to the (Navy/Marine Corps) mission have been evident throughout your career. I commend you for your outstanding professionalism, devotion and pride that you have exhibited during your (Naval/Marine Corps) service.

3. On the occasion of your discharge from active (Naval/Marine Corps) service, I express my sincere desire for your continued success and join with your many friends at (organization) in wishing you and your family the best possible future.

/Signature/

LOA – EXAMPLE # 3

From:
To:
Subj: LETTER OF APPRECIATION

1. During the period (date) to (date) you were attached to (organization). You were assigned to the (organizational element) as (job/billet).

2. With a keen sense of responsibility, you attained a high degree of expertise in your assigned duties. You further enhanced you value by constantly applying yourself to learning the many techniques and procedures used throughout (organization) and became proficient in numerous jobs normally assigned to more senior personnel. Additionally, you performed your additional duties of (list duties) in a manner as to bring credit to (organization) and the United States (Navy/Marine Corps). Your cheerful countenance and easy manner during periods of austere manning and demanding operational commitments was an additional asset to this command.

3. As you depart (organization) for duty (at command) it is with sincere appreciation that I congratulate you for a job WELL DONE. May fair winds and following seas always be with you.
/Signature/

LOA – EXAMPLE # 4

From:
To:
Subj: LETTER OF APRECIATION

1. During the period (date) through (date) you were assigned to (job), (organization). Throughout this period you displayed dedication and devotion to duty.

2. Your knowledge of and experience with (…) helped maintain the high state of operational readiness within (organization). During the time you were assigned, you planned and carried out a wide variety of projects to bring this (organization) to a higher state of material readiness. The overall effect of your performance led to (accomplishments). This was a direct result of your personal leadership and I commend you for this performance.

3. It is with regret that your tour of active duty with the United States (Navy/Marine Corps) is ending. I am sure that you will continue your interest in the (Navy/Marine Corps) in your future endeavors. On your departure you take with you the best wishes for continued success from everyone at (organization).
/Signature/

LOA – EXAMPLE # 5

From:
To:
Subj: LETTER OF APPRECIATION

1. It is with great pleasure that I convey my sincere appreciation for your efforts regarding the (event) on (date)..

2. Comments received from (…) were very complimentary and confirmed my own thoughts pertaining to the professional manner in which the (…) was planned and carried out. I know that it took long, hard hours of work and considerable personal sacrifice to correlate the myriad details necessary to ensure the success of (…). Your display of exceptional skill and resourcefulness in coordinating (…) are noteworthy. Your dependability, initiative, and talent to surmount difficulties led to (…). Your constant dedication and ability to complete tasks in a superior manner is a direct reflection of the respect and support you received from subordinates and seniors alike.

3. I applaud your accomplishments and extend to you my personal WELL DONE.
/Signature/

LOA – EXAMPLE # 6

From:
To:
Subj: LETTER OF APPRECIATION

1.   During the period (dates) you were assigned to the (organization) for duty. As (billet/title), a job normally assigned to (senior pay grade), your performance, across the board, was nothing less than OUTSTANDING.

2. You were responsible for (job highlights). The tireless hours you devoted to this task were instrumental to the timely completion of (…). Your contributions enabled (organization) to (list accomplishments).   You consistently demonstrated maturity, persistence, and a "can do" attitude rarely observed among your peers.

3. My personal thanks for a job WELL DONE.
                              /Signature/

LOA – EXAMPLE # 7

From:
To:
Subj: LETTER OF APPRECIATION

1.   During the period (dates) you were assigned to (organization) for duty. Your various assignments included (list jobs).

2.   Your individual performance and contribution to mission accomplishment in each and every assignment were OUTSTANDING.   You were selected over your peers for special recognition as (…). Your dedication and performance of duty throughout your tour at the (organization) have been most commendable.

3. As you prepare for separation from active duty, it is with sincere appreciation that I congratulate you for your honorable and faithful service. Having served with distinction in the most powerful (Navy/Marine Corps) the world has ever known, you have earned the right to say: "I served my country with pride." I am confident that the excellent traits you displayed at (command) will ensure your continued success in civilian life. Your many friends and I wish you continued success in all your future endeavors. We wish you fair winds and following seas.
/Signature/

LETTER OF COMMENDATION

From:
To:
Subj: LETTER OF COMMENDATION

1. Upon your transfer to the (Fleet Reserve/Retired List), I extend my personal gratitude and appreciation for your continuing faithful service to your country. You can be justifiably proud of your rewarding and patriotic career.

2. To aid you in reviewing your (distinguished/successful) career, the below is a listing of commands at which you honorably served.

You entered the service at (location) on (date) and have since served with the following commands:

> COMMAND   FROM   TO
> (Add commands and dates)

3. You earned a considerable amount of personal and professional recognition in your career, including the following official awards and decorations. (Add list.)

4. You, as much as anyone who has ever served, have helped foster and preserve the strong and honorable traditions of a

mighty United States (Navy/Marine Corps) that has helped defend and preserve the freedom that you, your fellow countrymen, and others throughout the free world continue to enjoy.

5. Your professionalism and loyal personal dedication to duty and country reflect great credit upon yourself and the United States (Navy/Marine Corps). In behalf of all of your shipmates, past and present, I wish you every success and happiness as you depart the Service.

/Signature/

SAILOR/MARINE OF THE (PERIOD)

The criteria for nominating individuals for recognition as Sailor/Marine of the Year, Quarter, Month, etc. are as many and varied as there organizations and individuals involved in the process.

In general, a write-up on an individual being nominated for Sailor/Marine of the (Period) should include personal and professional performance traits.

The write-up required at an individual command/unit is normally short and brief for two reasons. The first reason is to encourage seniors to take the time to recommend and nominate their top performers. The second reason is that a local screening board usually has the desire to personally interview everyone nominated. At this level of competition the results of the interview board usually carries more weight than the original write-up. Thus, when local commands/units forward the names of their nominees to higher echelons the supporting write-up must become more and more competitive and comprehensive. Geographic separation of lower echelon commands/units from higher echelons may prevent a personal interview of each individual nominated. As this level of competition is reached a screening board "narrows the field" of nominees using only the write-up. At this level, command employment and pride may also come into play.

When nominating someone for this special recognition, most of the justification should be in terms of what the individual accomplished during the period for which the nomination is submitted. It may be helpful to briefly note prior performance and accomplishment to show a continuing trend of superior effort and performance. Some screening board members may not be fully familiar with the particular work load, schedule, or environment of an individual's organization. If this is the case, be sure to briefly highlight pertinent facts and details. It is also a good idea to include a few well chosen personal traits (dependable, professional attitude, etc.).

When considering what information to put in the write-up, review the following subjects.

Job Performance	Command/Civic Involvement
Leadership	Off-Duty Activities
Technical Expertise	Innovative Improvements
Counseling Others	Secondary/Collateral Duties
Helping Others	Volunteering
Behavior	Military Professionalism
Personal Development	Helped Meet Organization Goals
Training Given/Received	Special Recognition Received
Appearance	Individual Initiative

Remember, there is not much difference in the text of a performance appraisal, an individual award, or a Sailor/Marine of the (Period) nomination. It might be helpful to review other sections of this book before writing your first draft of a Sailor or Marine of the (Period) input.

INTERVIEW SELECTION BOARD

If an individual is going to appear before a selection or screening board, it is a good idea for that individual's organization to hold its own selection board screening process. First, this gives the individual some practice at answering questions in a professional but familiar atmosphere. Second, the screening board members can critique the individual after the interview and offer ideas and suggestions for improving interview performance.

A person going before almost any interview board can be expected to be tense and apprehensive, especially because of the "unknown" elements. If other members of an organization have appeared before interview boards, it would be a good idea to have them team up with any inexperienced personnel and share some of their experiences. Explaining the routine and process of the selection board can have a calming effect on someone with little or no previous experience. Additionally, going over the types of questions that may be asked will increase self-assurance and personal confidence. Those are good qualities to present to a selection or screening board.

The questions board members ask are as varied and diverse as the members who sit on the board. There is no standard question list. Each member is free to venture into any area he or she may choose. "If you saw a close friend of yours taking drugs, what would you do?" "What do you think about the United States' policy on (whatever)?" Different people might give different answers to some questions, and all could be correct. Local interview board members, for the most part, want a candidate's thoughts, ideas and opinions on subjects. They are not looking for cut-and-dry "right" or "wrong" answers.

INTERVIEW BOARD HINTS

*Be straightforward, honest and sincere.
*Do not talk too fast or too slow.
*Do not talk with your hands (do not wave them around).
*Sit still. Do not squirm around.
*Keep eye-to-eye contact.   Use eye-to-eye contact when talking to board members. Do not look at only one individual. You are talking to the entire board, so share your eye contact (and answers) with all members.
*Appearance: Must be above reproach.   An excellent appearance always gives a person the inside track to selection.
*World/Military Events: Be prepared to discuss world and military events. Watch the news on television and read the newspaper. Know at least what's behind the headlines.

With the above "ground rules" covered, the following pages are provided to give ideas and examples on how to draft Sailor/Marine of the (Period) write-ups.

The first example attempts to show the total range and scope of an individual who is competing for selection at a high level. The remainder of the examples gives a variety of range.

SAILOR/MARINE OF THE PERIOD – NUMBER #1

(Name) is preeminently a (Navy/Marine Corps) man.   His personal involvement and commitment to the goals and ideals of the (Navy/Marine Corps) are without equal. In high school he voluntarily joined the Navy Junior Reserve Officers Training Corps (NJROTC), completing the three year program in two years, and attained the rank of Battalion (…). In Basic Training he was selected to lead his company as its (…).

During a recent decline in (organization) manning, (Name) accepted new challenges and volunteered for a workload that equaled or exceeded that of any other (peer group) at (organization). He was initially assigned the responsibilities of (…).   He launched himself into his new and unaccustomed duties with uncommon zeal and vitality. Immediately evaluating the jobs at hand, he set short and long range goals, restructured his available work force, and originated an ingenious and comprehensive management and supervisory control system. The system was an unqualified success and his work package was completed in half the allotted time.

(Name) volunteered for additional responsibilities. Each time he met the challenge and asked for an even larger share of the workload. Within a brief period of time he had assumed (number) of additional jobs, including (…) and (…). In his (…) duties he managed with flawless execution and attention to detail an (…) operation with a budget that exceeded (amount). His assignment to career counseling duties proved immensely successful; (number) of (number) eligible personnel reenlisted.

(Name) has a rich technical experience and a professional insight that exceeds (…). He identified and solved a number of operational discrepancies. His professional manner and organizational acumen allowed him to (…) with 100% efficiency and accuracy. Constructing a (…) from scratch and surveyed material, he saved the Navy (…) dollars.

(Name) was assigned to (organization) training duties because of his positive attitude, energetic personality, and his ability to inspire others. Additionally, he enrolled in college taking night classes in active pursuit of a Bachelor of Science degree in (subject). His professionalism and sterling personal example set the pace for his subordinates. Within (time), no fewer than (numbers) of his men and women were actively enrolled in college classes, proving once again that there is no substitute for leadership by example.

(Name) qualified as (…) Specialist during this busy operational period, becoming only one of (number) people to become so qualified.

Working unusually long hours to complete his myriad responsibilities did not detract (Name) from civic pride or involvement. He volunteered two weekends a month at a local church assisting in neighborhood rebuilding projects.

(Name) was able to accomplish much more than his peers because of his exceptional organizational keenness and his ability to work with and lead others. With a natural frankness and sincerity, he displays a deep concern for the feelings of others. These traits, his honesty, integrity and unparalleled professional competence generate immediate confidence in others.

In summary, (Name) has displayed a sustained superior performance without equal. He is that one individual in an organization whom superiors routinely rely on to supervise of solve difficult problems. His charismatic and cheerful attitude is infectious and spread easily throughout the ranks. The military presence he presents is of "recruit poster" quality. (Name) deep personal pride and inspirational leadership identify him as an exceptional career (peer group). (Command) is proud to nominate (Name) for (organization) Sailor of the (Period).

SAILOR/MARINE OF THE PERIOD – NUMBER #2

(Name) has been a valuable asset to (organization) throughout this selection period by voluntarily assuming direct responsibility for (...). Her masterful control of this entire evolution allowed others to concentrate their efforts in other areas of responsibility, thereby saving numerous man hours. Throughout this period she performed flawlessly and sacrificed significant personal time off. Through (Name) industrious efforts and self sacrifice, she initiated and implemented a plan to (...). This effort has been a definite asset to the successful operation of (organization) and a valuable tool and aid to (...).

Due to (Name) maturity and diligence she was charged with supervising the (...) Team which had responsibility for all (...). She performed these duties in an exceptional manner, keeping the (organization) ahead of schedule while an maintaining excellent quality of workmanship.

27

(Name) personal performance, industrious attitude, and devotion to duty are unsurpassed by anyone in her specialty. Additionally, she is successfully filling the position of (...), which historically has been assigned to someone two pay grades her senior. (Name) is a highly reliable individual who promotes high morale and good will. She is a model (Sailor/Marine) in behavior and attitude, and she provides an exceptionally high degree of leadership and supervisory ability.

It is with distinct pleasure that (organization) nominates (Name) for recognition as (...).

SAILOR/MARINE OF THE PERIOD – NUMBER #3

(Name) consistently performs his duties in an exemplary and highly professional manner, demonstrating superior performance and attention to duty. I believe that an individual must perform with excellence while on duty, and in addition, benefit himself personally and professionally outside normal work hours to be worthy of (Sailor/Marine) of the (Period). (Name) has met and exceeded all of these requirements and has earned my strongest endorsement for selection.

(Name) specific accomplishments include: (list accomplishments). Additionally, he conceived and implemented a comprehensive (...) program. He dedicated more than (...) hours of normal off-duty time on this project. His efforts resulted in a direct increase in operational efficiency.

(Name) has been taking off-duty college courses when (organization) operating schedule permits. To date he has completed (number) of courses with a grade point average of (...).

(Name) epitomizes those rare qualities most sought in today's military professional. He realizes that personal involvement and individual commitment are the cornerstones to any successful organization. Working with and understanding people are another one of his strong assets. He knows each subordinate's abilities and limitations, and integrates this knowledge into their daily activities. His uncommon maturity and common sense, coupled with his ability to apply the correct amount of diplomacy and direct tact, allows him to obtain the best possible results from others in any situation.

(Name) knowledge of his technical specialty, total dedication to duty, and willingness to assist anyone in any capacity has made him a valued member of (organization). No better representative for (Sailor/Marine) of the (Period) could be sought. He is most highly recommended for immediate selection.

SAILOR/MARINE OF THE PERIOD – NUMBER #4

(Name) current assignment as (…) requires a high degree of leadership skill, tact, and personal responsibility, all of which he possesses in abundance. In his job he provides direct leadership and guidance to (number) personnel in different technical fields. This organization is well organized and managed, and enjoys an unusually high degree of morale and pride in workmanship.

Though busy with the administration of an enormous number of personnel and equipment, (Name) manages to find time to become personally involved in resolving difficult maintenance problems. Very few weekends pass without him being called in to help correct some of the more serious problems. (Name) is dedicated to providing the best possible service twenty-four hours a day, seven days a week.

(Name) ability to comprehend and master the maintenance requirements of the most advanced (…) equipment through self-study and on-the-job training is overwhelming evidence of his technical superiority. He is an expert repairman on the (…) equipment despite not having attended formal schooling.

(Name) dynamic leadership, initiative, and overall professional performance set him apart from his peers. His day to day work and value to (organization) is head and shoulders above his contemporaries. (Name) is most strongly recommended for selection as (Sailor/Marine) of the (Period).

SAILOR/MARINE OF THE PERIOD – NUMBER #5

(Name) is a dedicated professional who strives for perfection in all endeavors. In all assignments she has demonstrated sound, mature judgment and flexibility not normally noted in someone of her paygrade. In addition to her normal duties of (…) she volunteered for assignment (to/as) (…) which routinely requires off-duty time to complete. In this capacity she performed with the highest degree of professionalism and dedication. She enjoys a full, busy work schedule and thrives on additional responsibility.

(Name) is interested in people and is continually involved in projects to promote the welfare of others. During this selection period she assisted in the preparation, operation, and maintenance of (…). She also participated in Project (…), an evolution designed to give the general public some insight into the importance of the functions and mission of (organization).

(Name) is a superb leader and manager. She uses tact and superior supervisory skills as a highly productive management tool in directing the activities of others. She displays a genuine concern for others and her "can do" attitude is a definite asset to (organization).

(Name) is highly deserving of consideration as (Sailor/Marine) of the (Period).

SAILOR/MARINE OF THE PERIOD – NUMBER #6

(Name) has consistently demonstrated an exceptionally high degree of military and professional excellence. His knowledge of rating, total dedication to duty, and willingness to assist in any capacity has made him a valuable member of (organization). His technical competence is unsurpassed. He has, on his own initiative, learned to operate and troubleshoot many (equipment/systems) for which he has received no formal training. First and foremost is his sound working knowledge and understanding of the complicated (...) system. By setting the example and making himself a technical source of information, he has helped influence others to higher professional achievement and development.

(Name) worth and value to (organization) extends beyond his outstanding technical competence. During a recent period when (organization) was severely undermanned, he was called upon to assume a position of greater responsibility as (...) Supervisor. Only his thorough understanding of (organization) operation and mission, his leadership skills, and his total willingness to help out in any capacity made this assignment both possible and successful.

(Name) spends off duty time going to night school at the University of (...) in pursuit of a degree in (...). Additionally, he has served as (organization) (...) key person, achieving superior results.

(Name) is deserving of serious consideration as (Sailor/Marine) of the (Period).

SAILOR/MARINE OF THE PERIOD – NUMBER #7

(Name) is extremely efficient and highly motivated. He displays superior talent and industry in completing all tasks. He is directly responsible for (...). Since he assumed these duties, two operational evaluations and three administrative inspections have been conducted by offices outside of this command. In each case his area of responsibility received an OUTSTANDING grade. The grades are directly attributable to (Name) personal initiative, dedication, and devotion to duty. At no time during his tenure as (job) has there been an operational outage or missed commitment due to the need for services in his area of expertise.

31

(Name) thoughtfulness and compassion for subordinates are tempered by fairness and concern. In his position of supervisor and counselor he displays the professionalism of a model (…).

(Name) is actively involved in the (organization) retention program. His off-duty hours are frequently filled with activities and events involving junior personnel, and he misses no opportunity to point out the advantages and benefits of a military career.

(Name) represents the excellence, spirit, and dedication of an ideal supervisor and leader. His concern, involvement, and consideration for others contribute directly to sustained high morale. (Name) is most qualified and deserving to earn the distinction of (Sailor/Marine) of the (Period).

SAILOR/MARINE OF THE PERIOD – NUMBER #8

(Name) has served as (…) since his arrival. He has kept himself cognizant of all matters pertaining to the management and operation of (…). Additionally, during this time he willingly accepted the added responsibility of (…) Supervisor and displayed consistently outstanding performance in that capacity.

Possessing exceptional organizational and planning abilities, (Name) has continually endeavored to improve the effectiveness of (organization). He has met with considerable success. He was quick to identify weak areas in (…) and took immediate and positive steps to improve these areas. Through his efforts and initiative, a more efficient method of maintaining accountability of (…) was instituted. To fully perform his job many hours of off-time were often required, yet (Name) was uncomplaining and gave willingly and freely of his personal time and energy. His unselfish devotion to duty has contributed much to the successful completion of (…) and was a contributing factor in receiving a grade of OUTSTANDING during a recent (…) Inspection.

Specifically, (Name) accomplishments include: *Revised and put in motion a new (...). *Revised and instituted new (...). *Drafted a comprehensive (...). *Conducted a complete review of (...), which resulted in a revision of existing policies.

(Name) is highly deserving of recognition as (Sailor/Marine) of the (Period) and is so recommended. He is, and will continue to be, a military model for others to follow.

SAILOR/MARINE OF THE PERIOD – NUMBER #9

(Name) military service has been highlighted by individual accomplishment and team contribution. He has a thirst for knowledge and an untiring desire for challenge. In addition to earning a (...) Degree, he has completed (...) military schools and (...) military correspondence courses. This education and his ability to apply that which he has learned have been invaluable in helping this organization meet all operational commitments with success. He performed admirably in a listing of jobs that would have overwhelmed his contemporaries. And, many of these jobs are routinely assigned to more senior people. Some of his major assignments and achievements include:
        *Organized (...)
        *Completed (...)
        *Qualified (...)
A person of lesser initiative and drive would have been overcome by these assignments. Nod only did (Name) thrive on this work, his leadership and (...) is these key responsibilities helped (organization) earn (...).

(Name) is most highly recommended for (Sailor/Marine) of the (Period).

SAILOR/MARINE OF THE PERIOD – NUMBER #10

(Name) is an exceptional career person whose performance routinely exceeds all requirements and expectations. Intelligent and conscientious, he requires neither motivation nor guidance in order to attain superior results. His performance during this selection period has been superior to the performance of (number) others as judged by a panel of his superiors. He has completed all requirements for (…) Supervisor and junctions superbly in that capacity. He has submitted recommendations to streamline operational procedures that have been incorporated into organizational policy and have since proven highly beneficial to (organization). On several occasions during a recent high tempo operational period he remained on duty long after the rest of his team was relieved to assist (…).

(Name) is a highly competent individual who has virtually mastered every aspect of (…) operations. He is a qualified (…) operator and supervisor. Extremely flexible, his leadership and maturity allows him to confidently make correct decisions related to (…). While on duty he is continually busy; however, he is never too busy to take the time to explain operational procedures and equipment operation to new or less qualified personnel. He is a patient and tactful individual, well liked by everyone who knows him. He is a pace-setter, the person others look to for leadership and guidance in professional and personal matters.

(Name) is an outstanding candidate for (Sailor/Marine) of the (Period).

SAILOR/MARINE OF THE PERIOD – NUMBER #11

(Name) possesses the human qualities of leadership and the professional technical expertise of a "top notch" supervisor. His adeptness in administering the proper combination of direction, encouragement, and discipline in supervising subordinates elicits their most positive and productive response.

(Name) has been the key individual in the command responsible for placing the (…) system into full operation. Spending many off-duty hours in training, he has attained an in-depth working expertise of this highly intricate and sophisticated system.

(Name) is friendly and has an active, outgoing personality. He is frequently called upon by subordinates and peers alike for advice in professional and personal matters. An active member of three civic organizations, he is committed to community involvement.

(Name) is not only an outstanding leader, but also a most dependable manager and administrator. Leading by example, he is always ahead of the game in managing his personnel and financial assets.

(Name) is currently attending night classes at the University of (…) where he has completed (…) courses and expects to earn his Associate Degree within the next (…) months.

(Name) noteworthy achievements as a military man, and his involvement in the community reflect credit upon his command and the United States (Navy/Marine Corps).

SAILOR/MARINE OF THE PERIOD – NUMBER #12

(Name) performs his assigned duties in a truly efficient, reliable, and professional manner. His resourcefulness and strong sense of professionalism are reflected in his every action.

Since reporting aboard (Name) has spent many hours of rigorous training to become fully qualified in (…) systems. Additionally, he has successfully completed an extensive locally administered written examination on the (…) system. His actions and efforts were instrumental to (organization) receiving a grade of "OUTSTANDING" during a recent technical evaluation conducted by (…).

(Name) is a highly motivated individual who possesses a positive attitude toward the military and continually displays an intense desire to serve in any capacity. He has shown great personal interest in his co-workers' welfare by submitting suggestions and in making improvements in the habitability of work spaces. He presents an extremely sharp and well groomed appearance, setting an outstanding example for others.

(Name) is actively involved in (organization) sporting activities. He is a member of the (…) and (…) sports teams. Other off-duty activities include civic involvement as a member of (…) and (…).

(Name) self-confidence and pride in the (Navy/Marine Corps) are readily apparent by his enthusiasm and zeal in completing any assignment. (Name) is an excellent candidate for (Sailor/Marine) of the (Period).

SAILOR/MARINE OF THE PERIOD – NUMBER #13

(Name) performance of duty has been absolutely outstanding. The technical skill and sound management practices he has displayed in planning, coordinating, and implementing the diverse requirements of (…) far exceed that normally expected of someone in his peer group. He was the first (…) to qualify under a new and rigorous (…) training program. To date, he is one of only two to hold those qualifications. He has, without question, gained the respect and confidence of his superiors.

In his collateral duty as career counselor, (Name) initiative and strong support for the (Navy/Marine Corps) has a career directly contributed to the impressive retention rates enjoyed by this (organization). He personally writes a letter to all new personnel before their arrival, introducing himself and explaining briefly his career counseling duties, and asks if there is any way that he may be of assistance. This personal touch is indicative of his thoroughness and dedication to this important duty. The next result of his effort has been an enhanced career retention program throughout (organization), and a positive, career-oriented climate.

(Name) is a leader and a positive force in initiating the planning for (organization) parties, social, and recreational events. He established (organization) intramural sports teams and fully supports all command sponsored activities.

(Name) is a dedicated (Navy man/Marine) whose military conduct and bearing are outstanding. I have personally commended him for his sharp appearance at formal personnel inspections. He is a "military professional" in the fullest sense of the term and meaning. I most strongly recommend (Name) for selection as (Sailor/Marine) of the (Period).

SAILOR/MARINE OF THE PERIOD – NUMBER #14

(Name) is an outstanding performer with a wealth of knowledge and experience in her technical specialty. She is an exceptional leader and is routinely selected to train new personnel, especially those without pervious formal (...) training. The results have been impressive, producing effective (...) that make contributions to mission accomplishment. The enthusiasm, sense of pride, and professional developed by trainees by (Name) are intangible benefits that are difficult to measure but which contribute directly to operational readiness and mission accomplishment.

(Name) honesty and integrity, coupled with her sterling professional competence and leadership ability, generate immediate confidence in her superiors and subordinates. Her sound knowledge of career programs and her desire to put these programs into action are considered prime assets to (organization) re-enlistment efforts. Because of her enthusiasm toward a successful career, she was recently appointed (organization) Career Counselor. She launched herself into these new duties with missionary zeal and vitality. On her own initiative, and because of her profound concern for others, she has made herself available twenty-four hours a day, seven days a week to any individual desiring information on career programs and patterns.

(Name's) outside activities are many and varied. As an exceptionally gifted sports person, she represented the (organization) in (sport) competition. As busy as she is on and off duty work and community involvement, she finds time to take evening classes at the University of (…). In the past year she has completed (…) semester hours of undergraduate study.

(Name) is an individual who is always on the move, always busy at her professional job or assisting others. In this exceptional example of a military professional there is seen an individual who is deeply moved with a career in the United States (Navy/Marine Corps). She would well represent (organization) as (Sailor/Marine) of the (Period).

SAILOR/MARINE OF THE PERIOD – NUMBER #15

(Name) demonstrates extraordinary professional ability on a daily basis. He has an uncommon perceptiveness to the morale and welfare needs of others. Since his assignment to (job), he has brought about significant improvement in all aspects of (…). Perhaps even more important than (Name's) outstanding professional performance is his thoughtfulness and compassion for his personnel. He displays the concern and professionalism of a model leader.

(Name) is an enthusiastic leader who believes that each individual should actively participate in all (organization) activities and events. Subordinates willingly follow his lead in these important morale building areas.

In military and civilian attire, (Name) is a paragon of excellent appearance and bearing. The even-tempered supervision of his personnel has made him an excellent leader.

In summary, (Name) represents the excellence, spirit, and professional dedication of a model career person. His concern and consideration for others is a mainstay of his personality. He refuses to be content with merely accepting the "status quo," and always finds ways and means of improving morale, team spirit, and pride. (Name) is most worthy of serious consideration as (Sailor/Marine) of the (Period).

SAILOR/MARINE OF THE PERIOD – NUMBER #16

(Name) has demonstrated a continuing high degree of professional excellence. His knowledge of his technical specialty, total dedication to duty, and his willingness to assist in any capacity has made him a valuable asset to (organization). Routinely assigned jobs given to more senior personnel, (Name) has made a name for himself by (…). His excellent use of the correct amount of tact and direct leadership is proving instrumental in promoting a feeling of pride and excellence throughout (organization).

(Name) personal charm and charisma are noted on a daily basis by his superiors and have earned him a deep sense of respect by all with whom he comes in contact. His desire and willingness to assist others was the motivating force in his selection as Chairman of the Command (…).

(Name) is a continual source of innovative ideas and suggestions. His affable personality and willingness to assist others in any capacity instills high morale and a strong sense of esprit de corps in those around him. He is held in high esteem by his superiors for his ability to adapt to changing situations and make sound, logical supervisory decisions.

(Name) has the attributes most desired of a (Sailor/Marine) of the (Period). He is most highly recommended for this honor.

SAILOR/MARINE OF THE PERIOD – NUMBER #17

Since being assigned to (organization), (Name) has demonstrated outstanding professional ability and leadership qualities by maintaining a superior level of technical expertise and operational proficiency. His inquisitive nature often results in new maintenance techniques that save manpower and money. He has rendered invaluable assistance to the training officer by helping produce training aids which resulted in better training and more proficient operations personnel.

(Name) consistently performs his duties with skill, eagerness, and ingenuity, and is extremely effective in guiding others in the execution of their duties. His leadership skills and managerial abilities have enabled him to mold a highly capable and professional unit.

During periods of personnel shortages, (Name) has been called upon to assume positions of added responsibility and in each case he responded admirably. The most notable example of this was his significant contribution toward a grade of "OUTSTANDING" received during a recent inspection by (...). Additionally, his leadership abilities have resulted in monetary savings and improved personnel habitability in work and living spaces.

(Name) is actively pursuing higher education. He has completed (...) semester hours through a local community college, working for a degree in (...).

(Name) has displayed a sustained superior performance of duty far above that of his contemporaries. He is a versatile, well-rounded technician. It is with pride that I nominate (Name) as (Sailor/Marine) of the (Period).

PERFORMANCE

APPRAISALS

PERFORMANCE

APPRAISALS

The sample write-ups in this guide reflect a variety of styles. They give the reader a variety of ideas on how subject material can be written. When drafting performance appraisals, remember that you are writing to "sell" the evaluee to selection boards by covering that individual's performance, ability, and potential.

There is enough material in this guide to form a sound base in the construction of hundreds of individual write-ups, each with its own uniqueness and individuality.

The material in one chapter of this book can be used with the subject matter of other chapters.

REMEMBER:
"If you do not know how to draft a performance appraisal, you do not know how to read one—your own included."

"If you cannot author a good narrative, you are hurting the careers of those individuals working for you who deserve to be promoted."

**FREQUENT USE OF THIS GUIDE WILL INCREASE
YOUR ABILITY TO UNDERSTAND
AND WRITE PERFORMANCE APPRAISALS**

INTRODUCTION

Every large organization has some means to evaluate the performance of its members. Administrators call this evaluation process a "performance appraisal."

PRIMARY OBJECTIVES OF GIVING PERFORMANCE APPRAISALS

1. To identify promotion, retention, and future duty potential.

2. To select, promote and retain the best qualified personnel.

3. To provide feedback to the evaluee.

PERFORMANCES MEASURED

1. PERSONAL TRAITS – How something is done (for example the leadership, initiative, etc. used or applied to accomplish something).

2. JOB PERFORMANCE – What and how much is done.

3. JOB BEHAVIOR – Appearance, adaptability, behavior, etc.

OBJECTIVE & SUBJECTIVE ANALYSIS

OBJECTIVE ANALYSIS should be used whenever possible to document an individual's performance. Objective analysis means to quantify performance results. How much was done? What was done? Use hours, time, percent, dollars, etc.

SUBJECTIVE ANALYSIS is the evaluator's perceptions, beliefs, or thoughts on how something was accomplished. This is an analysis of a person's "inner" qualities (or personality) and must be based on observations over a period of time. Subjective analysis is used to describe what prompted or caused an individual to do something (personal traits such as leadership, imagination, etc.).

PREPARATION CHECK-LIST

The more knowledge and tools an evaluator his at his or her disposal the better. The following information should be reviewed PRIOR to committing a subordinate's performance to print.

1. All performance appraisals should be handled discretely. They should be worked on in private.

2. Copies (or working copies) of past performance appraisals might be retained on file for reference for the next reporting period.

3. Insofar as practicable, reporting seniors should grade all performance appraisals of the same competitive category at one time. This will facilitate comparative grading.

4. Endeavor to obtain a just and equitable spread in the marks assigned to a comparative group.

5. Do not gravitate toward either a gratuitously high or rigidly severe policy of grading. The services are plagued by general over-assessment of average performers and occasional under assessment of "top performers." This serves to reduce the promotional opportunities of the "best qualified."

6. Exercise care to mark objectively, avoiding any tendency which might allow general impressions, a single incident or a particular trait, characteristic, or quality to influence other marks unduly.

7. When uncertain, due to limited observation, as to the appropriate evaluation of any rating area, mark "Not Observed" block rather than assign a "middle-of-the road" mark.

8. Avoid marking a new person somewhat lower than he or she deserves in order to reflect improved performance in subsequent performance appraisals. This malpractice can result in unjust advancement or assignment actions.

9. Before beginning to write, check over available performance date and determine which category you are going to place an individual being reported on:

   a. Head and shoulders above his contemporaries - promote early/now.

   b. Above many contemporaries – promote above most.

   c. Good performer – promote with majority of contemporaries.

   d. Behind peer group – do not promote.

When a decision has been reached, write a performance appraisal that will support and justify your position.

10. The "head and shoulders" performers should be immediately identified at the start of the narrative. The remaining write-up must justify and reinforce your position.

11. Ensure that realistic marks are assigned to individuals whose performance of duty has been manifestly unsatisfactory. Impersonal grading and concise statements of fact best serve overall interests under such circumstances.

12. Conversely, ensure that due consideration is accorded when an individual demonstrates truly outstanding or exceptional professional competence and potential. In such areas accentuate the positive. Be sure to state the major accomplishments that an individual achieved. More importantly, comment constructively on capacity or potential for future increased responsibility or promotion.

13. If the command has made an outstanding performance during the reporting period, an individual's personal contribution to this effect should be included. Of course, the converse is true.

14. After the completion of a performance appraisal, review prior reports or grades on the same person, if available, to ensure that any changes in the marks on the current report are intended. Any significant shift of marks in reports, especially when signed by the same reporting senior, should be substantiated in the narrative.

15. When making subsequent reports on the same person, guard against repetitive phraseology as this will reflect lack of thought on your part, and it will not help an individual's promotion chances.

16. Before submitting a smooth performance appraisal, analyze the narrative to make sure that what is meant to be said is, in fact, actually being said. Give careful thought not only to what the chosen words mean to the evaluator, but also how they may be construed by a selection board.

17. When the performance appraisal is finished, review it to ensure that:
    a. All parts are consistent (marks and narrative agree).
    b. The trend in performance (increase or decrease) is correctly conveyed.
    c. All spelling and grammatical errors are corrected.

18. Bear in mind that performance appraisal narratives reflect the degree and extent in which evaluators measure up to their moral obligation. And, an evaluator's write-up may be used to judge his or her performance.

19. Words are both valuable and dangerous tools. Choose them carefully.

20. Words mean what they say. Review the following:

POTENTIAL   CAPACITY   ABILITY
To indicate that an individual has these qualities without supporting evidence will register to a selection board as "insufficient data." A person can have POTENTIAL, CAPACITY, or ABILITY and yet accomplish nothing. Write how these qualities were demonstrated.

TRIES   STRIVES
Someone can TRY or STRIVE without accomplishing anything. As above, note how these qualities were positively demonstrated.

ACCEPTS ASSIGNED NORMALLY GENERALLY

Simply ACCEPTING assignments does not show initiative. Performing ASSIGNMENTS does not show initiative. NORMALLY and GENERALLY mean less than always.

ABOVE AVERAGE AVERAGE
EXCELLENT OUTSTANDING

These words have "canned" meanings and understandings. ABOVE AVERAGE is generally assumed to mean less than EXCELLENT or OUTSTANDING. AVERAGE means less than ABOVE AVERAGE, etc. If you are going to place someone's performance in one of these categories, be sure to choose the correct word(s).

"DO" Check List

-DO submit performance appraisals on time and in the correct format.
-DO write performance appraisals directed TO selection boards.
-DO write on how someone contributed above or below what is normally expected.
-DO write to express, not impress.
-DO be fair, honest, and objective.
-DO comment of growth potential and qualifications for advancement and future duty assignments.
-DO write on hard, pertinent facts, not "faint praises" without substance.
-DO use short, concise phrases or complete sentences with proper grammar.

"DON'T" Check List

-DON'T assign marks that are inconsistent with the narrative.
-DON'T write performance appraisals direct TO the individual.
-DON'T assign exceptionally high or low marks without comments in the narrative that clearly distinguish the performance.
-DON'T include minor, isolated, or insignificant imperfections which do not affect performance.
-DON'T use "glittering generalities" which go on and on without saying anything useful.
-DON'T use long words when shorter words will work.

47

-DON'T be verbose or redundant.

-DON'T restate the job description in the narrative. That space is too valuable.

-DON'T write "during the period of this report" or words to that effect. It is understood, unless otherwise stated, that all actions and events in a performance appraisal occurred during the reporting period being covered. Again, narrative space is too valuable.

-DON'T start too many sentences with the same: He… He… His… etc. Reading becomes sluggish and boring and shows lack of attention or ability on the part of the drafter.

-DON'T use a person's name without the associated rank. For example, do not write "Jones is…" instead, it should be "LT Jones is…" or "Seaman Jones is …" A performance appraisal is an official document and an individual's rank should always accompany his or her name.

-DON'T use the term "ratee."   It is too impersonal and impresses no one.

DRAFTING THE NARRATIVE

1. **OBJECTIVE.** Performance appraisals should be drafted with two objectives in mind. These objectives are:

a. To document, in SPECIFIC terms, what an individual contributed to command effectiveness and accomplishment; and,

b. To document the subjective "inner" qualities demonstrated by an individual on how performance was accomplished.

2. **GUIDANCE.**

a. BE POSITIVE.   Any shortcoming or deficiency mentioned in the narrative should be significant, either in terms of performance or potential. At any level in an organization some occasional, routine guidance is necessary.   If the commend it made that someone requires occasional instruction or guidance, that means that he or she requires more instruction of guidance than would normally be expected. In effect, comments on minor deficiencies are automatically magnified when they are included in the narrative.

b. BE CORRECT. A direct, hard-hitting write-up is better than an elegant one—concentrate more on content and specific accomplishments.

c. BE FACTUAL. Quantify individual achievements and accomplishments when possible.

d. BE SPECIFIC. A few well worded phrases of sentences on individual accomplishment and achievement mean much more than pages on billet description, command employment, etc.

e. BE OBJECTIVE. To the maximum extent possible, comment on quantifiable "objective" accomplishments, not on "subjective" personal notions.

OPENING FORMAT

The most closely read sentences in a performance appraisal are the opening sentences. The opening should be a powerful and persuasive statement—an "attention getter" to immediately capture the attention of the reader. The opening format can be limited to four themes:

a. Overview of best attributes/performance (or the converse for substandard performers.

b. Organizational ranking (especially for top performers.)

c. Potential (for top performers).

d. Awards or other forms of recognition received.

The opening format sets the "theme" for the remainder of the narrative.

OPENING FORMAT SAMPLES
(**Bullet Phrase Statements)

** A "bullet phrase statement" may or may not have a subject, object or verb.

(Name) is an exceptionally well qualified (…). Extremely well organized and mission-oriented. Infused (organization) with enthusiasm, team work, and dedication. Unlimited potential. Awarded (…) for (action).

(Name) professional talents, dedication, and aggressive work habits are an asset to (organization). Virtually unlimited potential. Awarded Letter of Commendation for (action).

(Name) is an outstanding manager and organizer. Willing to accept any assignment regardless of scope or size. Boundless potential. Selected as (…) of the Year.

(Name) is an energetic, industrious, and conscientious individual who has proven herself time after time to be a top performer. (Awards) (Potential).

(Name) has continually proven himself to be a (peer group) of exemplary character and outstanding ability. (Awards) (Potential).

(Name) professional knowledge, self-motivation, and determined efforts have made excellent contributions to the efficient functioning of (organization). (Awards) (Potential).

CLOSING FORMAT

The CLOSING FORMAT is another good place for a drafter to "sell" an individual to a selection board. Restating potential is a good way to end a performance appraisal.
>...Virtually unlimited potential
>Limitless potential
>Unbound potential
>Extraordinary growth potential

SUMMARY

Performance appraisal systems are relatively easy to understand. To properly draft one, simply refer to and follow the appropriate instruction(s). However, today there is keen competition for the limited number of available promotion slots. Writing a performance appraisal that just meets the instructional requirements by no means assures success or promotion. Proper use of the material available in this book can enhance promotion competitiveness.

NARRATIVE STRUCTURE SAMPLES
(Listed in no particular order)

(Name) is ready for positions of increased responsibility and trust now. Recommended for (...) duty. He is most strongly recommended for immediate promotion to (...).

(Name) is well read with a good working knowledge of the English language. The written reports he submits are clear and concise. His oral presentations command the complete attention of a listening audience.

(Name) rare and successful blend of leadership coupled with superior management and administrative abilities assure success in virtually any assignment.

(Name) stays with a job until it is completed, regardless of time of day or night. During the past three months he worked over 100 off-duty hours re-outfitting and organizing (...). Unlimited Potential. Highly recommended for (...) duty.

(Name) career continues to be underscored by pride, self-improvement and accomplishment. Initially assigned the primary duties of (...), he found time to assume other, equally demanding tasks. Filling in as the (...), he organized the monumental task of (...). In the area of (...), he personally planned and scheduled (...). Then he volunteered to assume the increased and diverse duties of (...). In this capacity he managed the successful efforts to (...).

(Name) is the most outstanding (peer group) at (organization). Top notch leader. Well versed in all facets of his professional specialty. Energetic and resourceful, he always plans ahead and stays ahead impending deadlines. A self-starter with great desire for professional challenge he leaves nothing to chance.

(Name) is a firm, fair, unbiased leader who demands high standards of performance from self and subordinates. Effectively capitalizes on subordinate strengths and improves weaknesses. He is a highly talented front-runner in peer group. Promote early.

The wide and varied technical background that (Name) brought to this (organization) were instrumental in starting the successful operation of (...). Being undermanned, the job was particularly demanding and time consuming. Working with others in a unified and cohesive manner is a particularly strong asset of (Name).

(Name) has the ability to immediately establish and maintain excellent rapport with others on all levels. Much of this is due to the fair, open, and unbiased manner of his leadership style. Each person knows that he or she will be given an equal opportunity commensurate with capabilities.

(Name) personally counsels each newly reporting person, setting forth organizational requirements and what the individual can expect in return.

(Name) communicates thoughts and ideas with ease and clarity. Written reports are brief, concise and to the point. Conduct and appearance are above reproach. He demonstrates a continuing pride in uniform and service. Instills this same pride in others.

(Name) is an industrious individual with great versatility, approaching all tasking enthusiastically and with dispatch. A skillful manager with proven ability to attain a high standard of performance, he is ready for promotion now.

(Name) directs others with firm but fair hand, without dulling their initiative. Readily adaptable to changes in policy or workload, he always gives a special effort to ensure cohesiveness and team work.

(Name) establishes good rapport with others and does not hesitate to provide personal or professional assistance. He encourages trust and team work through genuine interest in others. Accomplishments include (...).

(Name) watch team accomplished (...). He received written praise from (...) for ability to (...). A proponent of physical fitness, (Name) actively participates in various sporting events and maintains a trim physique. His conduct and appearance, on and off duty, are a model worthy of emulation by the entire (...) community.

(Name) fully enjoys military life and is quick to point out career benefits to others. He will not tolerate open dissent toward command policies or procedures. Personally responsible for convincing others to take off-duty educational courses and classes, (Name) himself has completed (...).

(Name) is the most productive and versatile (peer group) at (organization). A proven top quality organizer, administrator, and manager whose potential for increased responsibility and authority is boundless.

(Name) has a great deal of energy, is highly industrious, and does not believe in idle time. These rare qualities, coupled with his friendly personality and quick wit, allow him to establish and maintain an atmosphere of pride and professionalism in any organizational environment.

(Name) is eager to stay abreast of the latest changes in technology. Currently enrolled in (...). He is a top candidate for (...).

(Name) is a steadying and guiding influence to others. He is ready now to meet increased responsibility and challenge. He is most strongly recommended for promotion ahead of peer group.

(Name) is a poised and mature (peer group) with a thirst for knowledge and a desire for challenge. Soft spoken with an authoritative manner and commanding presence. A positive motivator who displays compassion and determination, he is able to (…). Intelligent and articulate he runs an orderly and highly productive organization.

(Name) is a self-starter whose great personal initiative and leadership skills identify him as being "head and shoulders" above contemporaries.

(Name) is a top performer with unlimited potential. Totally professional and poised, he is a self-starter with intelligence.   And, he always volunteers for additional responsibility.

(Name) is a rising superstar of boundless energy and potential.   He does not believe in idle time or unfinished projects, and he manages his own time and that of others to best possible advantage.

(Name) possesses managerial and organizational expertise rarely observed in (peer group).   He completes a large volume of work each day, frequently working extra hours.

(Name) is neat, trim and fit, presenting an immaculate "recruit poster" quality appearance. Articulate in speech, polite in manner.   He submits timely and accurate staff work. Enjoying the loyalty, cooperation and total support of subordinates, he is able to (…).

(Name) is ready for promotion now.   The superior management skill and leadership ability he possesses allows him to (…).   He is extremely knowledgeable, industrious, and totally resourceful.

(Name) performance is head and shoulders above her peers.   An original thinker, she thrives on challenge and responsibility.   She is particularly adept at gaining the immediate support and loyalty of others.

(Name) is an absolute top quality performer in his technical specialty.   He adds more to the job than is expected. And, he is continually alert for ways to increase efficiency and operational effectiveness. Personal and outgoing, he is a real morale booster.

(Name) is work-aggressive and highly productive, with an unlimited potential for professional growth. The knack he has for administrative detail is without equal. His enthusiastic "take charge" attitude promotes high morale throughout the ranks.

(Name) is an excellent all-around (peer group). Conscientious and totally dependable, he is able to (…). In tense or trying situations he can always be counted upon to provide the appropriate spark of leadership, humor, or energy.

(Name) is a proven ace (…) with endless potential and ability. He is energetic, industrious and conscientious. His outstanding performance (in/as) (…) contributed significantly to a high level of readiness enjoyed by (organization). He has a knack for getting the job done where others fail. Promote now.

(Name) is my number one (peer group). Promote ahead of others. His dedication and attention to detail are without equal. An energetic self-starter, he demands and receives only top quality performance from his subordinates. With a ready sense of humor and a pleasant personality, he fosters high morale throughout the ranks.

(Name) is an exceptional leader, manager, and organizer. His demonstrated performance as a leader has significantly improved the overall readiness of (organization). Pride and job accomplishment underscore his daily performance. A dynamic, compassionate leader, he knows how to motivate others.

WORD PICTURE

PERSONALITY

WORD PICTURE PERSONALITY

Documenting exactly what a person accomplishes in a performance appraisal is both useful and necessary. Work accomplishment alone, however, does not give a complete description of "picture" of an individual. The careful use of a few well chosen "word picture" words can describe a person's inner qualities—what possesses a person to do something, what a person "IS."

By combining what a person accomplishes and putting to print along with those accomplishments a person's personality characteristics, a complete "picture" of an individual is possible. Take, for example, the following:

"(Name) is energetic, resourceful, and self-reliant. He (go on to list exactly what he or she accomplished)."

In the above example, a selection board will know what was accomplished. More importantly, the board will gain valuable insight as to the individual's "inner" qualities, capabilities, and potential ("energetic," "resourceful," "self-reliant").

Selection boards do not promote people simply because they do a good job in their present pay grade. The potential to successfully discharge the greater duties and responsibilities of higher pay grades must be clearly in evidence. A person's "inner" qualities must be documented in performance appraisals.

By using the appropriate "word picture personality" characteristics listed on the following pages, selection boards can "see" and evaluate the full worth and potential (or lack thereof) of an individual.

FAVORABLE – WORD PICTURE PERSONALITY
ADJECTIVES

ACE	ADEPT	ADMIRABLE
ADROIT	AFFABLE	AGILE
ALERT	ALL-AROUND	AMIABLE
AMICABLE	APPEALING	ARTISTIC
ASSERTIVE	AUSPICIOUS	CANDID
CHARISMATIC	CHARMING	CHEERFUL
COMPOSED	CONGENIAL	CORDIAL
COURAGEOUS	COURTEOUS	DETERMINED
DEVOTED	DEXTEROUS	DIPLOMATIC
DISCREET	DISTINGUISHED	DYNAMIC
EAGER	EFFERVESCENT	ELEGANT
ENERGETIC	ENTERPRISING	ENTHUSIASTIC
ETHICAL	EXCEPTIONAL	EXPERIENCED
EXPERT	EXUBERANT	FEARLESS
FORTHRIGHT	FRANK	FRIENDLY
GALLANT	GENEROUS	GRACIOUS
GREGARIOUS	GUNG HO	HONEST
HONORABLE	IMPOSING	INDUSTRIOUS
INFLUENTIAL	INNOVATIVE	INSPIRED
JUDICIOUS	LEVELHEADED	LIVELY
LOYAL	MANNERLY	MASTERFUL
MATURE	METICULOUS	NOBLE
OPENHANDED	OUTGOING	PEERLESS
PERSUASIVE	PLEASANT	POLISHED
POLITE	PROFICIENT	PROGRESSIVE
PROMINENT	PROUD	RELIABLE
REPUTABLE	RESPECTED	RESOURCEFUL
SELF-COMPOSED	SINCERE	SKILLED
SKILLFUL	SOCIABLE	SPIRITED
STALWART	STELLAR	STERLING
STUDIOUS	SUAVE	TACTFUL
TIDY	TRUSTWORTHY	TRUTHFUL
UNFLAPPABLE	UP-AND-COMING	UPRIGHT
VERSATILE	ZEALOUS	ZESTY

FAVORABLE – WORD PICTURE PERSONALITY
NOUNS

ACCLAIM	ACCOLADE	ACHIEVER
AGILITY	ADEPT	CHARISMA
COMPETITOR	COURAGE	DETERMINATION
DEXTERITY	DIGNITY	DIPLOMACY
DIPLOMAT	EAGER BEAVER	EAGERNESS
ELEGANCE	ENTHUSIASM	EPITOME
ESPRIT DE CORPS	ESTEEM	EXPERTISE
FINESSE	FLAIR	FORTITUDE
FRIENDLY	GIFT	GLORY
GOODWILL	GRIT	HONESTY
HONOR	HUMOR	INDUSTRY
INFLUENTIAL	INITIATIVE	INSPIRATION
INTEGRITY	LOYALTY	MASTERMIND
MATURITY	MOTIVATION	PILLAR
PROFESSION	PROFESSIONAL	SPECIALIST
TACT	VITALITY	ZEAL

FAVORABLE – WORD PICTURE PERSONALITY
VERBS

ACCLAIM	ADMIRE	CHAMPION
CHARM	ENCOURAGE	ENGENDER
ENHANCE	ENTRUST	EPITOMIZE
EXALT	EXCEL	EXEMPLIFY
MOTIVATE	OUTCLASS	OUTDO
OUTMATCH	OUTSHINE	OVERSHADOW
PERSONIFY	POLIS	PRAISE
PREVAIL	RESPECT	SPIRIT

OF OR WITHIN THE MIND

The following list of words express, define, state, or describe FAVORABLY individual intellect, intelligence, knowledge, wisdom, or reasoning.

ADJECTIVES

ABLE	ACCOMPLISHED	ACUTE
AGILE-MINDED	ALERT	ANALYTIC
ASTUTE	AWARE	BRIGHT
BRILLIANT	CALCULATING	CAREFUL
CLEVER	COGENT	COMMON SENSE
COPREHENSIVE	CRAFTY	CREATIVE
CULTIVATED	CULTURED	CURIOUS
DEXTEROUS	DISCERNIBLE	DISCREET
EDUCATED	ENLIGHTENED	FARSEEING
FARSIGHTED	FERTILE	GIFTED
IDEAL	IMAGINATION	IMAGINATIVE
INCISIVE	INNATE	INFORMED
INGENIOUS	INSIGHTFUL	INSPIRATION
INTELLECTUAL	INTELLIGENT	INVENTIVE
JUDICIOUS	KEEN	KEEN-WITTED
KNOWLEDGEABLE	LEARNED	LETTERED
LOGICAL	MATURE	MENTAL
METHODICAL	MINDFUL	NIMBLE
PENETRATING	PERCEPTIVE	POWERFUL
PRAGMATIC	PROFICIENT	PROFOUND
PRUDENT	QUICK	RATIONAL
REASONABLE	RETENTIVE	SAGACIOUS
SENSIBLE	SHARP	SKILLFUL
SMART	STUDIOUS	TALENTED

OF OR WITHIN THE MIND
NOUNS

ABSTRACT	THOUGHT	ACUITY
ACUMEN	APTITUDE	APTNESS
ACUTENESS	BRAINCHILD	BRILLIANCE
CLEVERNESS	COGNITION	COGNIZANCE
COHERENCE	COMMON SENSE	CRAFTINESS
CREATIVE ABILITY	CREATIVENESS	CREATIVITY
CUNNING	DEDUCTION	EXPERIENCE
EXPERTISE	FACULTIES	FACULTY
FERTILE MIND	FREETHINKER	GENIUS
HEADWORK	IDEA	IMAGINATION
INGENUITY	INSIGHT	INSPIRATION

60

INTELLECT	INTELLECTUAL	INVENTIVENESS
INVENTOR	JUDGMENT	KEENNESS
KNOWLEDGE	LEARNING	LOGIC
MASTRY	OUTLOOK	PERCEPTION
PROFICIENCY	PRUDENCE	QUICK WIT
RATIONALITY	REASON	REASONING
RECALL	RESOLVE	RETENTIVITY
SCHOLAR	SENSIBILITY	SHARPNESS
SOUNDNESS	TALENT	TECHNIQUE
THINKER	TALENT	VISION
WISDOM	WIT	WITTICISM

OF OR WITHIN THE MIND
VERBS

COGITATE	COMPREHENT	CONCEIVE
CONCENTRATE	CREATE	DISCERN
ENLIGHTEN	ENVISION	FABRICATE
FORSEE	IMAGINE	INVENT
ORIGINATE	OUTTHINK	OUTWIT
PENETRATE	PERCEPTIVE	PONDER
POSTULATE	PRODUCE	RATIONALIZE
REASON	SAVVY	SPECULATE
TEACH	UNDERSTAND	VISION

SPEAKING AND WRITING

The following list of words express, define, state, or describe FAVORABLY an individual's ability or capacity to convey information and thoughts to others through the mastery of the English language.

ADJECTIVES

ARTICULATE	CLEAR-CUT	CONCISE
CONVERSANT	ELABORATE	ELOQUENT
EMPHATIC	EXPLICIT	FAIR-SPOKEN
FLUENT	IMPLICIT	INFORMATIVE
LUCID	SUCCINCT	TACIT
TERSE	WELL-SPOKEN	

NOUNS

CLARITY	DICTION	DISCOURSE
ELOQUENCE	LUCIDITY	ORATOR
QUIP	VERBALISM	WORDPLAY
WORDSMITH		

VERBS

CONFUTE	EDIT	EDITORALIZE
EDUCATE	ELUCIDATE	EMPHASIZE
ENUCIATE	EXPOUND	INSINUATE

HUMANE QUALITIES

The following list of words express, define, or describe how an individual inter-relates with others.

ADJECTIVES

BENEVOLENT	COMPASSIONATE	CONGRUOUS
EMPATHETIC	EMPATHIC	FEELING
FORGIVING	GENIAL	GENTLE
GREATHEARTED	HARMONIOUS	HEARTFELT
HOSPITABLE	HUMANE	KIND
KINDLY	NICE	OPENHEARTED
POIGNANT	REGRETFUL	RESPECTFUL
SELFLESS	SENSITIVE	SYMPATHETIC
TENDER	THOUGHTFUL	TRUSTFUL
UNSELFISH	WARM	WARMHEARTED

NOUNS

AMENITY	COMPASSION	CONSONANCE
CORTESY	EMPATHY	FAIR PLAY
FORGIVENESS	HARMONY	HUMANITARIAN
MERCY	NICETY	SENSITIVITY

VERBS

EMPATHIZE	FORGIVE	SYMPATHIZE

ADJECTIVES

BIG-HEARTED	COMPASSIONATE	EMPATHETIC
FEELING	FORGIVING	GENIAL
GENTLE	GOOD-HEARTED	HARMONIOUS
HEARTFELT	HOSPITABLE	HUMANE
KIND	KINDLY	NICE
OPENHEARTED	RESPECTFUL	SELFLESS
SENSITIVE	SYMPATHETIC	TENDER
THOUGHTFUL	TRUSTFUL	TRUSTING
UNSELFISH	WARM	WARMHEARTED

NOUNS

AMENITY	COMPASSION	COURTESY
EMPATHY	FORGIVENESS	HARMONY
HUMANITARIAN	NICETY	SENSITIVITY

VERBS

EMPATHIZE	FORGIVE	SYMPATHIZE

POSITIVE – ACTIVE or ACTION WORDS

ADJECTIVES

ABSOLUTE	ACCOMPLISHED	AGGRESSIVE
ARDENT	ARDUOUS	AUDACIOUS
BANNER	BOLD	CHALLENGING
COMPELLING	COMPTITIVE	COMPLEX
COMPLICATED	CONSUMMATE	CONVINCING
CRITICAL	CRUCIAL	DECISIVE
DIVERSE	DOMINANT	DOMINEERING
DRAMATIC	EFFICIENT	ELEVATED
ENVIABLE	ENVIOUS	ESSENTIAL
EXACT	EXACTING	EXCEEDING
EXCELLENT	EXCITING	EXEMPLARY
EXPEDIENT	EXTENSIVE	EXTREME
FABULOUS	FANTASTIC	FAR-REACHING
FAULTLESS	FIERCE	FIERY
FINE	FIRST-RATE	FOOLPROOF

FOREMOST	FRESH	FRUITFUL
GRANDIOSE	GRUELING	HEADLONG
HIGH-POWERED	HIGH-PRESSURE	IDEAL
ILLUSTRIOUS	IMMACULATE	IMPASSIONED
IMPECCABLE	IMPORTANT	IMPRESSIVE
INCREDIBLE	INEXHAUSTIBLE	INFALLIBLE
INFECTIOUS	INSATIABLE	INSTRUMENTAL
INTEGRAL	INTENSE	INTRICATE
LAUDABLE	LAUDATORY	MARVELOUS
NOTABLE	OUTSTANDING	PARAMOUNT
PERFECT	PERSISTENT	POSITIVE
POTENT	POWERFUL	PRECISE
PROSPEROUS	PUNCTILIOUS	PURPOSEFUL
QUICK	REFRESHING	RELENTLESS
REMARKABLE	RESILIENT	RESOUNDING
ROBUST	SERIOUS	SEVERE
SHIPSHAPE	SPEEDY	SPLENDID
SPOTLESS	STAGGERING	STIMULANT
STRENUOUS	STRICT	STRINGENT
STRONG	STRONG-WILLED	STUPENDOUS
SUBSTANTIAL	SUCCESSFUL	SUPERB
SUPERFINE	SUPERIOR	SUPERLATIVE
SUPPORTIVE	SUPREME	SURPASSING
SWIFT	TENACIOUS	TERRIFIC
THRIFTY	TOUGH	ULTIMATE
UNBEATABLE	UNBOUNDED	UNEQUIVOCAL
UNERRING	UNFAILING	UNPARALLELED
UNSTOPPABLE	VALUABLE	VIGILANT
WELL-DONE	WELL-ROUNDED	WELL-TIMED
WIDE-RANGING	WONDROUS	WORTHFUL
WORTHWHILE	WORTHY	

NOUNS

ACHIEVEMENT	APEX	ASSET
BRAINSTORM	CATALYST	COMMENDATION
COMPLEXITY	COMPLIMENT	CONTRIBUTION
DIEHARD	DRIVE	EMBODIMENT
EMULATION	ENCOURAGEMENT	ENDEAVOR
ENERGY	ENJOYMENT	ENTERPRISE

EXCELLENCE	EXCITEMENT	EXPEDIENCE
EXPERIENCE	EXUBERANCE	FEAT
FIRST	FIRST CLASS	GRANDEUR
HEADWAY	IDEAL	IMPETUS
IMPORTANCE	IMPROVEMENT	INCENTIVE
INFLUENCE	INNOVATION	KEYNOTE
KUDO	LANDMARK	MASTERY
MERIT	PASSIONATE	PERFECTION
PERSONIFICATION	PLAUDIT	POTENCY
POWER	POWERHOUSE	PRECISION
PREMIUM	PROGRESS	PROPSERITY
PROTOTYPE	QUALITY	RESILIENCE
SACRIFICE	SPARK	SPEARHEAD
STIMULUS	STRENGTH	SUCCESS
SUPERLATIVE	SUPREMACY	SWIFTNESS
TANACITY	THRIFT	VITALIZATION

VERBS

ACHIEVE	ADVOCATE	ANALYZE
ANTICIPATE	APPLAUD	ASPIRE
ASSERT	BOLSTER	CAPITOLIZE
COMMEND	CONCEIVE	CONTRIBUTE
CREATE	DEVISE	DOMINATE
EMERGE	EMBODY	EMULATE
ENERGIZE	ENFORCE	ENRICH
ENTHUSE	ESTABLISH	EXCEED
EXCITE	EXPEDITE	EXPLOIT
EXPLORE	FACILITATE	FINE-TUNE
FORMULATE	FORTIFY	FULFILL
GENERATE	HONE	IGNITE
IMPRESS	IMPROVE	IMPROVIZE
INITIATE	INNNOVATE	IMPROVE
INFUSE	INITIATE	INNOVATE
INSTILL	INVIGORATE	LAUNCH
NOURISH	ORGANIZE	ORGINATE
OVERCOME	OVERSEE	PERSEVERE
PERSIST	PREPARE	PROPEL
PROSPER	RECTIFY	REHABILITATE
RENEW	RENOVATE	RESURGE

REVIVE   SCRUTINIZE   SPARK
SPEARHEAD   STIMULATE   STRENGTHEN
SURPASS   THRIVE   ZENITH

BULLET

PHRASES

BULLET PHRASES

A "bullet phrase" is a statement that may or may not have a verb, object or subject. Bullet phrases serve to reduce the amount of space required to make a statement. Thus, using bullet phrases allows more material to be covered in the same amount of space, or the same amount of material in less space, than in formal sentence structure.

FORMAL SENTENCE EXAMPLE
"He is highly intelligent, possesses a stimulating imagination, and routinely provides sound advice and recommendations for anticipated problems."

BULLTE PHRASE EXAMPLE
"Highly intelligent, stimulating imagination, provides sound advice and recommendations."

The samples in this chapter are in bullet phrase form. They can be combined or used independently. The samples can be shortened more, or they can be turned into complete sentences.

BULLET PHRASES – FAVORABLE

PERSONAL, PERSONALITY TRAITS

...Perceptive and alert

...Cheerful personality

...Interesting, convincing speaker

...Courteous nature

...Calm and composed

...Projects air of dignity

...Great raw ability and talent

...Energetic spirit

...Talented and charismatic

...Great mental grasp

...Optimistic outlook

...Stimulating intelligence

...Calm and affable manner

...Interesting conversationalist

...Personal magnetism

...Broad and varied intellect

...Always enthusiastic

...Friendly and cheerful

...Strong moral fiber

...Sound of mind and judgment

...Sensitive and understanding

...Thoughtful and caring

...Quick to act

...Determined and dedicated

...Honest, respectful

...Contributes innovative ideas

...Intrepid, resolute drive

...Agreeable, pleasant personality

Keen sense of ethical conduct

...Sharp mental keenness

...Admired courage of conviction

...Clear, orderly self-expression

...Resilient personality

...A quick thinker

...Exceptional orator

...Uncommonly likable

...Thirst for knowledge

...Powerful, influential

...Alert, energetic

...Humorous and witty

...Emotionally stable

...Impeccable character

...Open minded

...Mentally alert

...Quick to learn

...Mental sharpness

...Bold, forward thinker

...Amiable, good natured

...Great personal drive

...Creatively inclined

...Firm and resolute

...Sound judgment

...Pleasing personality

...Never gives up

...Resourceful and dedicated

...Capable of independent decision

...Innovative and imaginative

...Advanced knowledge

...Optimistic outlook and attitude

...Correct mental approach

...Personal vision and courage

...Unlimited learning capacity

...Quick, penetrating mind

...Dominating force

...Cleverness and guild

...Stands on principles

...Proper behavior

...Clear in thought

...Sound, prudent judgment

...Even tempered

...Endless zeal and courage

...Relentless drive

...Well-calculated actions

...Highest integrity

...Frank and forward

...Frank and forward

...Honest and faithful

...Strong drive

...Matchless ingenuity

...Highly motivated

...Good common sense

...Extensive knowledge

..."Can do" enthusiasm

...Analytical mind

...Boundless energy

...Intellectual courage

...Plans ahead

...Exceedingly articulate

...Strong will

...High ethical principles

...Caring attitude

...Engenders trust

...Well organized

...Brilliant, lively wit

...Alert and energetic

...Keen rational powers

...Vision and foresight

...Astute and alert

...Adapts with ease

...Relentless drive

...Confident of abilities

...Strong spirit

...Boundless enthusiasm

...Great personal courage

...Organized and industrious

...Exercises sound judgment

...Stimulating imagination

...Full of energy

...Results oriented

...Pride and self-assured

...Well-adjusted

...Grasps essentials quickly

...Mentally alert

...Courage under pressure

...Thoughtful of others

...Emotionally stable

...Retentive mind

...Persuasive talker

...Great self control

...Matchless desire

...Unflagging zeal

...Keen sense of humor

...Self-motivated

...Discriminating mind

...Pillar of strength

...Emotionally mature

...Inquisitive mind

...Sparks excitement

...Strongly motivated

...Probing personality

...Mental courage

...A winning spirit

...Great foresight

...Great verbal dexterity

...Articulate speaker

...Resilient and energetic

...Kind manner

...Boundless ability

...Devotion to duty

...Genuine concern for others

...Unwavering self-reliance

...Impeccable moral character

...Winning spirit

...Elegant manner

...Positive attitude

...Engaging personality

...Intellectually gifted

...Creative writing ability

...Keen analytical abilities

...Dynamic personality

...Proper, correct manner

...Full of energy and ability

...Alert and energetic

...Artful and skillful

...Effervescent personality

...Good academic aptitude

...Energetic personality

...Inspiring imagination

...Cheerful personality

...Refined personality

...Vision for the future

...Eager and capable

...Forward-thinking

...Skilled innovator

...Confident of abilities

...Thorough thinker

...Good-natured & friendly

...Commanding presence

...Firm and resolute

...Sound moral character

...Cordial and affable

...Exudes optimism

...Clear vision of future

...Exacting by nature

Unselfish and trusting

Kind, amiable disposition

...Friendly and sociable

...Fighting enthusiasm

...Logical priorities

...Eager willingness

...Coverts ideas into action

...Highly motivated achiever

...Strong sense of purpose

...Exercises mature judgment

...Meticulous attention to detail

...Pillar of high moral purpose

...Good intellectual energy

...Puts ambition to good use

...Good judgment and foresight

...Aggressiveness of a zealot

...Keen intellectual perception

...Stays calm and collective

...Always a positive attitude

...Talented and charismatic

Ethical, honest personality

...Energetic, resilient personality

...Unrestrained enthusiasm

...Confident manner

...Strength of character

...Well groomed

...Large vocabulary

...Kind disposition

...Never shows despair

...At ease in any situation

...Unshakable character

...Gives quality results

...Articulate in speech

...Fosters goodwill

...Resourceful manner

...Positive mental attitude

...Fresh, new ideas

...High personal integrity

...Clear, analytical mind

...Firm and fair

...Original thinker

...Mental dexterity

...Terrific sense of humor

...Courage of conviction

...Stimulating conversationalist

...Decisive and determined

...Fine sense of moral prudence

...Commanding in presence

...Vast intellectual capacity

...Mentally quick and alert

...Endless zeal and courage

...Intelligent with an orderly mind

...Great personal industry

...Ready wit, outgoing personality

...Alert and responsive

...Always ahead of the action

..."Can do" attitude and amicable personality boosts morale.

Progressive outlook, resilient and resolute personality

...Never looses sight of important events or developments

...Analytical mind, adaptable to changing situations.

...Good Samaritan, dedicated to helping others

...Few people work harder or have more innate talent

...Intellectually gifted, technically experiences, always highly motivated

...Enchanting personality

...Great personal initiative

...Graceful in manner

Thoughtful and caring

...Completely self-reliant

...Unbeatable character

...Good mental agility

...Impeccable character

...Take charge attitude

...Even temperament

...Quick mind

…Articulate in self-expression and innate ability to think logically

…Probing personality, quick to pick up on things

…Extremely friendly and sociable nature

…Sorts out pertinent facts and finds logical conclusions

…Effective in relating point of view and in winning an unbiased listener

…Possesses mental courage to stand on principles

…Dedicated, results-oriented individual

…Acts responsibly in all situations

…Relentless drive and dedication in all endeavors

…Superb speaker who can instill teamwork and cooperation

…Indestructible sense of humor

…Good ability to learn and understand

…Sound in thought, good in judgment

…Unlimited capacity for solving difficult problems

…Uses proper blend of personal candor and sound professional judgment

…Clear and logical in thought

…Skilled, eloquent speaker

…Strongly motivated to succeed

…Courage of character to forge ahead

...Exceptional professional competence

...Finest qualities of moral strength

...Long-standing record of dedication

...Uses common sense to tackle problems

...Logical in decision making process

...Intelligent, inquisitive, and confident

...Originates well thought out ideas

...Does not wait for direction to proceed with task at hand

...Noteworthy demeanor and presence

...Understanding and genuine concern for welfare of others

...Presents succinctly and eloquently prepared briefs

...Presence of mind to act correctly in critical situations

...Exceptional drive and energy

...Analytical thought process

...Daily actions marked by efficiency and practical logic

...Flexible and cooperative under any conditions

...Earned wide praise for total professionalism

...Impressive initiative and motivation

...Personal demeanor without equal

...Drive and motivation is refreshing

...Innate ability to get to crux of any problem

...Fully capable of meeting new situations

...Strength of character to tackle any assignment

...Abundant energy and enthusiasm

...Will and courage to succeed, despite any tasking

...Highest standards of integrity and loyalty

...Unmatched capacity for learning

...Strong desire and ability to learn

...Sees through difficult problems and finds solutions

...Polished, persuasive speaker

...Innate ability to grasp and understand perplexing matters

...Exercises sound and logical judgment

...Inspires self-improvement through sterling personal example

...Faces demanding challenges head-on

...High sense of personal pride

...Bubbling enthusiasm permeates entire organization

...Thoughts are well written and orally expressed

...Never in doubt or confused

...Abundant initiative and personal drive

...Rational and logical to all tasking

...Amicable, friendly disposition

…Enthusiasm and demeanor are noteworthy

…Clear and positive in self-expression

…Mentally quick and resourceful

…High ethical principles

…Highly perceptive intellect

…Sound, sensible judgment

…Refined presence and dignified manner

…Great intellectual awareness

…Demonstrates sound, mature judgment

…Articulate in speech and the written word

…Learning ability and growth potential unlimited

…Innovative and productive

…Pursues new ideas with success

…Friendly, radiant personality

…Always coming up with something better or improved

…Enjoys mental challenge of resolving complex problems

…Highly accurate, professionally written reports

…Fully developed sense of loyalty

…Unending urge and drive for success

…Boundless capacity for work

…Makes best use of available resources

...Great personal drive and energy

...Keeps composure under pressure

...Amicable personality spiced with good wit and humor

...Thrives on pressures of immediacy

...Responds to trying situations with innovative suggestions

...Interesting speaker, convincing conversationalist

...Highest standards of loyalty and integrity

...Cheerful and good-natured

...Curious and inquisitive nature

...Courteous and respectful nature

...Personal commitment to professionalism and excellence

...Always willing to volunteer

...Wide diversity of professional talent

...Resourceful and respected

...Cooperative and cheerful

...Feeds on adverse conditions others would shun

...Capable of independent decision and action

...Outstanding attitude and morale builder

...Impeccable moral character

...Imaginative and inventive mind

...Loyal dedication to duty

...Polishes, persuasive speaker

...Strong advocate of equal opportunity

...Fair and without prejudice

...Well mannered with pleasant personality

...Mind is quick and decisive

...Not easily excited under stress or pressure

...Eager and interested in professional matters

...Unequaled academic accomplishments

...Strong drive toward professional excellence

...Constant source of innovative, workable ideas

...Highly respected professionally

...Logical and correct courses of action

...Unquenchable thirst for knowledge

...Contributes innovative, workable solutions to problems

...Mentally skillful and unhesitant in action

...High morality and ethical principles

...Refreshing, lively personality

...Utmost degree of accuracy

...Practical, prudent wisdom

...Orderly and rational reasoning

...Stable in character, resolute in action

...Composes in stressful situations

...High moral principles and personal values

...Seeks personal growth and development

...Methodical and highly conscientious

...Takes initiative for additional responsibilities

...Work marked by initiative and excellence

...Dependable with uncompromising principles

...Pillar of moral strength and courage

...Impressive breadth of experience

...Dignified in presence and appearance

...Innovative and creative mind

...High ambition and achiever

...Well rounded with diverse talent

...Copes well in stress-filled circumstances

...High moral standards

...Strives for professional development

...Tremendous personal courage

...Endless constructive mental energy

...Highly developed sense of responsibility

…Keen sense of fair play

…Communicates ideas with ease and clarity

…Fair, open-minded in reason and action

…Friendly personality, quick wit

…Stable, well-adjusted personality

…Prompt in response to difficult situations

…Mentally alert and physically ready

…Quick and decisive in action

…Makes independent, correct decisions

…Affable, pleasant personality

…Studious, perceptive, and active mind

…Mannerly, courteous, and polite

…Clear analytical mind.

…Impeccable moral character

…Imaginative and inventive mind

…Steadfast, loyal dedication

…Polished, persuasive speaker

…Strong advocate of equal opportunity

…Creative thinking and innovative problem solving abilities

…Written products are clear and cogent

…Mind is quick, innovative and decisive

…Keen intellectual perception

…Composed, not easily excited under stress or pressure

…Highest personal integrity

…Eager and interested in all professional matters

…Constant source of innovative, workable ideas

…Ready wit and an outgoing personality

…Capable of orderly and rational reasoning

…Calm and composed disposition

…Continually seeks personal and professional development

…Methodical and highly conscientious

…Takes initiative for additional responsibilities

…Work marked by initiative and excellence

…A pillar of moral strength and courage

…Impressive breadth of experience

…Completely self-reliant

…Vast intellectual capacity

…Innovative and creative mind

…Well rounded individual with diverse talent

…High moral standards

…Endless energy, positive spirit

…Tremendous personal courage and self-discipline

…Highly developed sense of responsibility

…Fair and open-minded

…Fine sense of moral prudence

…Stable, well-adjusted personality

…Mentally alert

…Quick and decisive in action

…Logical and coherent mind

…Unselfish dedication to duty

…Intellectually productive

…Fully developed purpose and sense of pride

…Exercises sound judgment in practical matters

…Confident and composed under pressure

…Decisive in mind, determined in action

…Meets challenges beyond range of contemporaries

…Courage and determination in face of adversity

…Proven ability to lead

…Strong will and ability to succeed

…Self-confident of abilities

…Unassailable personal integrity

…Pleasant manner and personality

...Responsive to all tasking

...Always proper in manner and behavior

...Strong loyalty and sense of duty

...Positive, cooperative spirit

...Sensitive to needs of others

...Social grace

...Straightforward and above board

...Uses initiative to get things done

...Calm and controlled under trying conditions

...Sincere manner and caring nature

...Always proper mental attitude

...Inquisitive mind, exacting nature

...Abundance of zeal and enthusiasm for all tasking

...Intelligent with an inquisitive mind

...Full of vigor and ability

...Magnetic charm and appeal

...Great initiative and persistence

...Well developed sense of judgment

...Well adjusted mentally

...Mentally quick and resourceful

...Energetic with no wasted actions

...Strong personality and will

...Willing to stand up for principles

...Never lacking in spirit or exuberance

...Ideas well organized and thought out

...Ceaseless devotion to duty

...Good sense of humor and compassion

...Keeps clear mental picture of goals and objectives

...Without bias or prejudice

...Polite and elegant manner

...Sound decision making facilities

FAVORABLE

LEADERSHIP, MANAGEMENT, & ADMINISTRATION

...Sound management procedures   ...A real motivator

...Arouses and excites interest   ...Inspires others

...Molds character and courage   ...Stirs the imagination

...Creative management initiatives   ...Composed leader

...Exemplifies ideal leader   ...Fosters goodwill

...Firm, resolute leader   ...Bolsters spirits

...Promotes sound leadership   ...Good organizer

...Accomplished counselor

...Takes charge, a real leader

...Prompt, diligent administrator

...Inspires top performance

...Astute money manager

...Skillful, direct leadership

...Spirited, determined leader

...Astute, experienced leader

...Inspires and encourages

...Unparalleled leadership

...Motivates and leads others

...Instills pride and purpose

...Well-rounded leadership

...Recognizes top performers

...Meticulous administrator

...Encourages professional pride

...No-nonsense leader

...Knows success is team effort

...Concerned, caring leader

...Personal leadership magic

...Always an inspiration

...Exciting leader

...Firm leader

...Natural team leader

...Adroit administrator

...Positive motivator

...Firm, yet fair leader

...Real morale booster

...Promotes teamwork

...Accomplished leader

...Respected by others

...Leads by example

...Inspires greatness

...Morally fair and just

...Stirs up enthusiasm

...Charismatic leader

...Uncommon leader

...Agile leadership

...Inquisitive leader

...Interested in others

...Impressive leader

...Frank, direct leader

...Solid material manager

...Accomplished counselor

...Has "follow me" confidence

...Propagates goodwill

...Vigorous leadership style

...Promotes esprit de corps

...Innate managerial skills

...Engenders trust and confidence

...Runs cohesive organization

...Fully taxes subordinates

...Generates self-confidence

...Tactful leader and motivator

...Engenders self-development

...Capacity to lead others

...Sound leadership principles

...Exuberant, enthusiastic leader

...Thinks and acts rationally

...Outstanding rapport with others

...Always gets quality results

...Inspires confidence

...Unifying presence

...Selfless leader

...Imposing presence

...Positive influence

...Motivates others

...Team leader

...Stirs the imagination

...Instills loyalty and pride

...Inspires others

...Inspires the imagination

...Supports self-dignity

...Take-charge individual

...Polished, mature leader

...Manager extraordinary

...Careful, exact planner

...Inspiring enthusiasm

...Successful leader

...Accomplished manager

...Industrious manner

...Enviable punctuality

...Strong leadership attributes

...Inspires zeal and confidence

...Popular among peers

...Calm, patient leadership

...Error free production

...Quality leader

...A real morale booster

...Strong, decisive leader

...Exceptional manager and organizer

...Sincere concern for subordinate development

...Acts decisively in stressful situations

...Generates positive attitude and esprit de corps

...Alert and perceptive, prompt to act

...Experienced, knowledgeable manager

...Energetic personality, stimulating leader

...Accurate and careful about detail

...Prudent, economical use of resources

...Skillful employment of available resources

...Has a special flair for expert management of assets

...Individual vitality and "can do" spirit

...A "leader by example" who obtains superior results

...Helps individuals recognize self-dignity

...Displays uncommon leadership and enthusiasm

...Extremely perceptive and hard working

...Takes charge and makes positive things happen

...Wins support and maximum effort of others

...Molded efficient, well run organization

...Dedicated to betterment of subordinates

...Enjoys high morale and low discipline rate

...Invigorating supervisor and leader

...Always contributes 110% to team effort

...Excites and arouses others to action

...Fosters harmony and teamwork

...Exceptionally fine administrator

...Strict, firm and fair leader

...A dynamic leader who achieves maximum success

...Unified and coherent management philosophy

...Arouses enthusiasm and interest in others

...Breathed new life into a declining organization

...Strong aptitude for administrative work

...Has a firm grip on management principles

...Meticulous record keeping

...Timely submission of all reports

...Equitable and impartial leadership

...Established a professional work environment

...Exhibits high trust level in others

...Takes charge and gets things done in a timely manner

...Places mission first and personal interests second

...Quick to identify problems and apply correct fix

...Instills pride and dignity in others

...Keen managerial abilities

...Met diverse and demanding situations with ease

...A morale builder to every member of the organization

...A dynamic leader and vigorous worker

...Genuine concern for welfare of others

...Dedicated to mission purpose and accomplishment

...Direct, hard-line leader with unifying character

...Sets an example anyone would do well to follow

...Encourages trust through genuine personal interest

...Artful management of resources

...Superb manager of material and people

...Capitalizes on individual strengths of others

...Epitome of tactful leadership

...Stimulates subordinate professional growth

...Intense, compassionate leader

...Strict application of discipline leadership

...Brings out best in subordinates

...Loyalty and leadership to the chain of command

Personification of a dynamic and caring leader

...Ideally suited for top management positions

...Positive attitude generates enthusiasm at all levels

...Provides corrective, positive counseling

...Achieves unusually high standards of performance

...Proven ability to get things done

...Professional attitude radiates to others

...Good sense of organization

...Spontaneous propensity to leadership

...Reputation for dependable results

...Informed leader who genuinely cares about others

...Sets stringent but achievable performance standards

...Outstanding professional and supervisory ability

...Extremely versatile leader

...Concerned, caring leader

...Earns personal trust and confidence of others

...Treats others with dignity and self-respect

...Economically sound management practices

...Good leader, creates excitement and enthusiasm

...Establishes and pursues clear-cut goals

...Fair, impartial treatment of others

...Calm, methodical leadership with good results

...Skillful direction of others

...Concerned with the welfare of others

...Exceptionally adept at administrative matters

...Thoroughly proficient and efficient manager

...Keeps organization on an even keel

...Provided vital, positive leadership

...Artfully leads subordinates

...Skillful in leading others to desired goals

...Leadership merits special praise

...Provides an inner drive that motivates others

...Nurtures subordinate professional development

...A catalyst of team work and high morale

...Earned admiration and respect of others

...Embodies finest qualities of leadership

...Creates and maintains confidence and respect of others

...Shares considerable talent with others

…Demands and receives only the best from others

…Interacts harmoniously with others

…Gives others strong sense of direction

…Unending ability to generate enthusiasm in any tasking

…Quick to offer constructive advice to subordinates

..Strong professional drive for excellence

…Aggressive and imaginative management acumen

…Able and capable leadership

…Admirable blend of tact and direct leadership

…Potent and productive supervisor

…A demanding leader who gets impressive results

…Fosters unity and pride throughout the ranks

…Well developed, positive counseling techniques

…Fosters unparalleled productivity

…Provides valuable solutions to complex problems

…Inspires subordinates to put forth their best effort

…Personal contribution to morale has been most welcomed

…Calm and stable leader in crisis situations

…Engenders trust and confidence

…Superb leadership and unbridles enthusiasm

…Vigorous, work-aggressive leadership

...Astute manager of all assets

...Radiant, confident leader

...Highly respected leader and organizer

...Contributed immeasurably to high morale

...Superb leadership, unequaled performance

...Maintains excellent rapport with others

...Guiding and steadying influence on subordinates

...A master at providing direction and tactful leadership

...Proven leader with unbound potential

...Bold, imaginative leadershlp

...Commendable results in trying leadership situations

...Maintains an atmosphere of pride and accomplishment

...Poised and mature leader

...Positive results regardless of tasking difficulty

...Superior knowledge of administrative matters

...A proponent of strong, solid leadership

...Energizing and stimulating leadership

...Considerate leader who gets results

...A dominating influence in any organization

...Provides positive guidance that improves subordinate skills

...Great faculty for executing command decisions

...Provides skillful direction to others

...Impressive ability to motivate others

...Ignites the human spirit

...Provides assertive, positive leadership

...Allows subordinates to grow to fullest potential

...Persuasive and tactful leader

...Innate managerial skills

...Ingrained pursuit of excellence

...Leads with intensity, force, and energy

...Exceptional enthusiasm demonstrated on a daily basis

...Unrelenting commitment to job accomplishment

...Stands head and shoulders above others in leadership

...A standard bearer for excellent leadership

...A highly motivated leader

...Impressive record of management accomplishments

...Makes most effective use of available resources

...Sets and achieves long-rang goals and objectives

...Made visible impact on morale

...Great ability to lead

...Stimulates creative effort and work of others

...Delegates responsibility wisely and successfully

...Provides timely recognition for superior performance

...Develops subordinates at a rapid pace

...Makes optimum use of assigned personnel

...Keen sense of responsibility for individual rights

...An inspiration to each member of this organization

...Firmly and fairly enforces rules and standards

...Increased operational efficiency and effectiveness

...Never too busy to lend a helping hand to others

...Measurable improved overall operation performance

...Commands the fullest respect and support of others

...Fosters high morale and a total winning attitude and spirit

...Instills constructive loyalty up and down the ranks

...Extremely well liked and respected

...Ability to manage an incredible number of ongoing jobs

...A steadying influence to others

...Knows how to lead people and where to lead them

...Inspires others in a common effort and goal

...Good ability to coordinate group effort

...Unparalleled level of performance

...Responsive to needs of others

...Unwavering support of organizational goals

...Endless ability to meet mission requirements

...Creates favorable attitude and work environment

...Instills motivation in others with relative ease

...Provides resolutions to a wide range of problems

...Helped mold organization into a cohesive unit

...Positive and distinctive leadership

...Establishes and enforces clear-cut goals

...Demands positive results

...A take-charge individual

...Strong initiative and infectious enthusiasm

...Natural team leader

...Mainstay of character and strength

...Leads a proud team of professionals

...Leadership and faith to lead people successfully

...Personifies leadership by example

...Contributes immeasurably to morale and team effort

...Improved organization quality and efficiency

...Exceptional leadership and initiative

...Unsurpassed excellence

...Cornerstone of leadership and management success

...Always gives others a helping hand

...Efforts and resourcefulness inspires others

...Great effort toward mission accomplishment

...Management abilities led to real manpower savings

...Dynamic individual and leader

...Led the best trained group to new highs

...Remains stable and calm during crisis situations

...Puts mission accomplishment ahead of personal matters

...Outstanding managerial talent

...Instills loyalty and team effort in others

...Recognizes and rewards top performers

...Takes full advantage of subordinates' abilities

...Authoritative in action with a commanding presence

...Gets to the heart of any problem in short order

...Established a team spirit with a "can do" attitude

...Expert at drafting official correspondence

...Has good leadership abilities and determination

...Ignites enthusiasm throughout the ranks

...Exercises leadership in an exemplary manner

...The personification of a model leader

...Unflagging zeal and dedication

...Impressive manager and leader

...Unfailing devotion to duty

...Established and maintained a high state of morale

...Personal touch in leadership motivates others

...Gives a common purpose and vision to others

...Gained the respect and admiration of others

...Excellent staff work, leaves nothing to chance

...Highest caliber of leadership

...A master of positive leadership

...A leader of dynamic character

...Exceeded all tasking requirements

...Created and maintained excellent work environment

...Cultivates team work and a winning professional attitude

...Uses considerable managerial skills to best advantage

...Secures the energy and loyalty of others

...Makes positive things happen

...Not content with anything less than 100% effort

...Arouses the competitive spirit in others

...Sound leadership and management principles

...Highly capable leader

...Radiant personality with confident leadership abilities

...Sparks a spirit of job excitement in others

...Propagates goodwill and a desire for excellence

...Radiant energy and zeal quickly picked up by others

...Potent, productive leader

...Balanced blend of strong leadership and compassion

...Fully taxes each individual's capabilities

...Ready for more challenging and demanding positions

...Consistent quality of excellence

...Ideally suited to work with today's young professionals

...Continually searches for ways to raise efficiency

...Highly beneficial management abilities

...Enlightened leadership arouses best effort of others

...Accomplished counselor

...Exudes spirit of confidence and determination

...Innovative and decisive style of leadership

...Maintains a professional work environment

...Highly successful in obtaining maximum results

...Outstanding performance in a broad operating spectrum

...Exercises sound leadership principles

...Keenly aware of the personal side of leadership

...Concerned and caring leader

...Provides the spark that drives others to action

...Exemplary management acumen

...Leadership has considerably enhanced readiness

...A unifying presence to any organization

...Instills sense of pride and purpose in subordinates

...Sound judgment and leadership

...Projects image of a strong, steady leader

...A real motivator

...Knows how to stir the imagination of others

...Exceptionally effective in personnel leadership

...Remarkable ability to manage diverse operations

...Sound management practices and principles

...Dedicated leader

...Highest quality integrity

...Takes the lead in actively supporting chain of command

...Personalized style of leadership is highly effective

...Encourages subordinates to set high goals

...Own enthusiasm infiltrates the ranks

...Intolerant of mediocre performance

...Leads subordinates to desired level of performance

...Organizational harmony and team work without equal

...A real leader

...Always gives 100%

...Demands the best from others

...Contributes significantly to high morale

...Exceptionally well organized

...Contributed immeasurably to sustained superior performance

...Has a keen sense of good leadership principles

...Accepts each task with a positive, can do attitude

...Inspires high morale and esprit de corps among others

...Always contributes maximum ability to team effort

...Enforces a strong chain of command

...Persuasive and tactful leadership style

...Helps subordinates grow and creates a team spirit

...A leader of uncommon perceptiveness

...Special knack for bringing out the best in others

...Superior leadership across a broad range

...Recognizes that success is a team effort

...Helps others grow professionally and personally

...Not content with anything less than maximum effort

...Solid leader and manager

...Leads others in a straight and direct course of action

...Recognizes and rewards top performers

...Encourages professional development at every opportunity

...Desire for excellence contributed to organization excellence

...Obtains exceptional performance from subordinates

...Impressive ability to motivate others

...Contributes full measure to team effort

...Organization functions like a well oiled machine

...Optimistic outlook and "can do" enthusiasm

...Inspires others to put forth their best effort

...Has an enthusiasm for any and all challenges

...Knows how to use leadership to achieve an objective

...Tactful, considerate leader

...Infectious positive leadership attitude

...Continuing willingness to help others

...Routinely goes out of way to assist others

FAVORABLE

PERFORMANCE

…Totally committed to excellence

…Gives full effort

…Enterprising, intense performer

…Hard working

…Finds and fixes problems

…Competitive spirit

…Plans carefully and wisely

…Stands above peers

…Intense dedication to duty

…Reaches new heights

…Sound professional judgment

…Always volunteers

…Work free of mistakes

…True team player

…Takes wise courses of action

…Exceptional ability

…Maintains high standards

…Unparalleled success

…Steadfast dedication

…Stands above peers

…Dramatic and exciting

…Positive, fruitful future

…Highest standards

…Constant vigil

…Great technical curiosity

…Prompt and proper

…Gives an extra dimension

…High achiever

…Exhibits professional accuracy

…Considerably advanced

…Strong professional pride

…Unblemished record

…Proficient and industrious

…Up and coming star

…Seeks challenging assignments

…Smooth and flawless

...Acts decisively under pressure

...Sets professional example

...Delivers wholehearted support

...Overcomes all obstacles

...In-depth technical knowledge

...Impressive accomplishments

...Head and shoulders above peers

...Decisive in action and deed

...Premier performer

...Highly respected

...Reliable and dependable

...unrelenting work habits

...Achieves positive results

...Enjoys stressful situations

...Highest caliber work

...Capacity to meet challenges

...Proficient and effective

...Benchmark of excellence

Performs at peak efficiency

...Prompt and proper action

...Meets diverse challenges

...Accustomed to success

...A top professional

...A standard bearer

...Ace technician

...Thrives on challenges

...Prompt in response

...Superior to others

...Steady, faithful service

...Unblemished record

...Gives extra effort

...Clear cut goals

...Achieves desired ends

...Dominating force

...Action oriented

...Hard working

...Tireless worker

...Mission oriented

...Makes things happen

...A role model

...Gets positive results

...Bright, on the ball

...Quick to take positive action

...Captures the imagination

...Keen technical abilities

...Reached full potential

...Technically advanced

...Makes good things happen

...Decisive, action oriented

...Complete professional

...Comprehensive technical skill

...Impressive performer

...Springs into action

...Extremely competent

...Abundantly productive

...Uncommon excellence

...Skillful undertaking

...Prompt and responsive

...Responsibilities discharged superbly

...Actions always consistent with command policy

...Past performance and future potential all positive assets

...Unequivocal commitment to mission accomplishment

...Work aggressive

...Uses time wisely

...A driving force

...Without equal

...Hard charger

...Banner performer

...Durable and adaptable

...Prolific performer

...Promising newcomer

...Tough competitor

...Thoroughly proficient

...Stellar performer

...Exerts total effort

...Quick to respond

...Promotes new ideas

…Ability to accomplish diverse tasking with success

…Dedicated and highly competent

…Approaches each task with a positive attitude

…Accomplishes the most demanding tasks

…Enthusiastically tackles any tasking

…Achieves quality results

…Accepts additional responsibilities

…Superlative contributions and achievements

…Contributes maximum effort

…Provides timely advice and guidance

…Highly competent and dedicated

…Quality performer in any tasking

…Skilled in all areas of technical specialty

…Long history of devotion to duty

…Always puts forth quality effort

…Continues to improve on an already impressive record

…Exemplifies true meaning of "pride and professionalism"

…Starts early, works smarter and harder than peers

…Strong sense of duty highlights daily activities

…Successfully faces all challenges

…Has strong desire to succeed

...Takes charge and makes positive things happen

...Works well independent of direct supervision

...Flexible and cooperative when dealing with others

...Superlative contributions to mission accomplishment

...Resilient and energetic

...Has an abundance of inspiration for any tasking

...Energetic and highly motivated

...Straight line of dedication and inspiration

...Good abilities across the board

...Performance highlighted by uncommon quality

...Unusually high level of technical expertise

...Actively seeks additional responsibility

...Unfailing support of organizational policies

...Astute management of monetary and equipment assets

...Adapts to any situation with quality results

...Has a spirit of confidence and a relentless drive

...Refuses to be satisfied with anything less than full effort

...Ability and desire to assume broader scope of duties

...Highly motivated and hard working

...Superior performance routinely displayed

…Thrives on important responsibilities

…Keen technical insight

…Efficient performance highlights daily effort

…Always gives support to superiors

…Intense worker who is highly capable

…Diligent and persistent

…Aggressively tackles many demanding challenges

…Performs well under stress and pressure

…Quality performer with a bright future

…Completes all jobs on time or ahead of schedule

…Skill and resource to accomplish most difficult tasking

…Does not get stopped by obstacles

…Insatiable appetite for increased responsibility

…Highly self-motivated

…Job accomplishment is always number one priority

…Time-tested ability to get the job done

…Abilities beyond range and scope of peers

…All work performed with exacting quality

…Finest technical skill and knowledge available

…Routinely exceeds highest professional standards

…Epitomizes the model, career person

...Superior record of accomplishment

...Proven leadership abilities

...Exhibits the skill and reliability of a true professional

...Dynamic and positive approach to everyday problem solving

...Sets the course and speed for peers

...A front-runner in every category

...Impressive breadth of experience within technical specialty

...performs well in all situations

...Uses sound judgment to solve difficult problems

...Professional performance without peer

...Exceeds every requirement of assigned responsibilities

...Considers no job too difficult

...Takes every assignment as a personal challenge

...Trains for readiness and the unexpected

...Always ahead of the action

...Uncanny ability to find and fix problem areas

...High achiever, always attains desired results

...Takes corrective action without awaiting direction

...Made substantial and quality contributions

...A quality performer

…Always on the ball and ahead of peers

…Does what has to be done without waiting for guidance

…Relentless drive and motivation

…A "hot runner" with unlimited potential

…A true team player

…Enormous professional abilities

…Hand-picked for difficult and complex assignments

…Selfless devotion to duty and professionalism

…Steadfast performance and dedication to duty

…In-depth knowledge of technical specialty

…Unsurpassed devotion to duty

…Assumed more and more responsibilities with success

…Provides valuable solutions to difficult technical problems

…Takes advantage of every opportunity to improve

…High level of personal and professional expertise

…Upholds highest levels of pride and professionalism

…Enthusiastic response to any tasking

…Exceeds highest expectations

…Delivers wholehearted support in any assignment

…Most impressive thoroughness and attention to detail

…Continually seeks more challenging assignments

...Highest standards of a well-rounded professional

...Exceptional degree of accuracy and professionalism

...Boundless enthusiasm and ability

...A top professional in every sense of the word

...Rare ability to radiate enthusiasm in any tasking

...Energetic personality with a "can do" attitude

...Pride in job accomplishment highlight daily performance

...Performance and professionalism well above peers

...Exceptional results across the board

...Uses vast technical knowledge to maximum advantage

...Performance far exceeds peer group

...Always meets all stated objectives

...Increased overall operational effectiveness

...Experienced journeyman in technical specialty

...At the pinnacle of professional excellence

...Standard bearer for pride and professionalism

...A zealot in performance of any tasking

...Pursues all assignments with zeal and purpose

...Always takes pride in doing the best job possible

...Gets things done by taking the initiative

…Great sense of responsibility for quality of work

…Vast experience and technical know how

…Made major contributions to operational effectiveness

…Work of considerable and lasting value

…Completes all tasking in a truly professional manner

…An irreplaceable source of professional knowledge

…Exercises sound judgment

…Symbolizes a top professional

…Career underscored by pride and self-improvement

…Sets the standards by which excellence in measured

…Executes tasking expediently and correctly

…Possesses an infectious positive attitude

…Great ability to cope with difficult, tying situations

…Responsive to short-fused tasking and special assignments

…Forward-looking individual with many abilities

…Ready for positions of higher trust and responsibility

…Gives complete and energetic support to superiors

…Overwhelming willingness to tackle difficult tasking

…Enhances high morale

…Impressive record of accomplishments

…Diligent and persistent worker

...Introduces progressive new ideas that work

...Exhibits a high technical excellence

...Stimulates harmony and team spirit

...Keen technical abilities

...Unsurpassed devotion to duty

...Always sets the example

...Dedicated to mission purpose

...Vast technical experience

...Initiates sound new ideas

...Always provides whatever assistance required

...Contributes to high standards of excellence

...Impressive list of individual accomplishments

...Top professional in every respect

...Clearly exceeds all standards of excellence

...Coordinates diverse events with uncommon accuracy

...Sets and achieves high professional standards

...Surmounts problems and gets results

...Highly industrious

...Does not believe in idle time

...Aggressive and meticulous in completion of tasks

...Intolerant of mediocre performance

...Performance regularly exceeds job requirements

...Highly skilled in all phases of job

...Aggressive in solving developing problems

...Always productively employed

...Accepts challenges with alacrity

...Unfailing performance to duty

...Achieves quality results

...Unyielding drive and desire for success

...Enjoys total professional diversity

...Puts forth an unrelenting effort

...Places job ahead of personal interests

...Workload is correctly balanced and prioritized

...Exceptionally high level of performance

...Quick to provide personal effort on special projects

...Plans and completes an ambitious workload

...Top achiever in any task assigned

...Excels in every facet of technical specialty

...Job aggressive and dedicated

...All tasking completed in a commendable fashion

...Professional contributions are noteworthy

...Highly respected for technical expertise

...Carries out all demanding responsibilities

...Highly professional with a capable manner

...Submits timely solutions to a variety of problems

...Forward minded with work aggressive performance

...Gives considerable talent and effort to task at hand

...Exceptionally well organized

...Performance always exceeds expectations

...Uncompromising professionalism

...Proven top quality organizer

...Performance stands out among peers

...Exudes confidence and team spirit

...Sets the example for others

...Accomplishes difficult assignments with ease

...Enterprising and talented in technical specialty

...Overcomes adversity and gets the job done

...Devoted to professional excellence

...Confident of professional abilities

...Long list of impressive accomplishments

...Aggressively pursues difficult challenges

…Remarkable versatility and capability

…Prompt and correct in action

…Professional excellence rarely observed within peer group

…A real competitor

…Takes pride in a job well done

…Self-sacrificing, a real team player

…Demonstrates ultimate standards of excellence

…Tackles difficult tasking with joyous exuberance

…Accomplishes much more than others

…Plans are well organized and thought out

…Intense drive and determination

…Unafraid of long, hard work

…Sets and achieves high goals

…Persevering and enduring in completing all tasking

…Always timely, placing a premium on punctuality

…Never caught off guard or unprepared

…Accepts added responsibility

…Vigorously tackles any assignment

…Completes all assignments with accuracy and dispatch

…Proven technical specialist

…Discharges responsibilities with complete professionalism

…Highest standards of dedication and determination

…Accepts all responsibilities without wavering

…A self-starter

…Natural ability and aptitude for technically oriented tasks

…Carries out assignments to complete satisfaction

…Inspires a sense of purpose and teamwork

…Unswerving allegiance to duty

…Unrivaled professionalism

…Determined and dedicated professional

…A fruitful career ahead

…Routinely receives high acclaim and praise

…Attains quality results in any endeavor

…Highly skilled and well trained

…Frequently sought out for expert opinion

…Boundless energy

…Sets highest standards of excellence

…Eagerly accepts work others would avoid

…Adapts to varying situations with uncommon ease

…Ability to think logically

…Intense dedication and enthusiasm

…Has well defined plans and goals

…A model for all to emulate

…Extremely energetic and helpful

…Stimulates productive activity

…Always in vigorous pursuit of excellence

…Actions always conform to expected standards

…A first-rate professional

…Has a reputation for meeting all challenges

…Has professional excellence and a winning spirit

…Takes positive action without waiting for direction

…Puts forth extra effort when needed

…Work in impressive

…Resourceful and dedicated in all tasking

…Has a personal commitment to quality performance

…Capacity to meet challenges head-on

…Aggressive in assumption of additional responsibility

…A multi-disciplined individual with a promising future

…Proficient and industrious in performance of duty

…Long-standing record of professional accomplishment

…Will not retreat in the face of adversity

…Technical skill and ability know virtually no bounds

...Uses time wisely with no wasted energy

...Seeks opportunities for professional growth

...Consistently produces outstanding results

...Every goal met in a timely manner

...Displays keen interest and ability in all tasking

...Actions well planned and smoothly executed

...Attains positive results regardless of complexity

...Plans ahead and is never pushed to meet a deadline

...Always gives serious and determined effort

...Completes all assignments with dispatch

...Rates first against all competition

...Almost infinite growth potential

...Tremendous capacity for professional growth

...Committed to achieving high goals

...At the zenith of technical specialty

...Makes decisions after weighing all pertinent facts

...Enforces and supports regulations and superiors

...Ingrained ability to achieve positive results

...Succeeds under stress and pressure

...Refuses to give up in face of adversity

...Works hard to make the jobs of others easier

...Achieves highest level of performance

...Well rounded knowledge of technical specialty

...Maintains superior rapport with everyone

...Uniformly outstanding results

...Possesses all attributes needed to excel

...concise understanding of technical specialty

...Gives total support to team effort

...Supports and enforces all rules and regulations

...Designs plans that contribute to overall success

...Top performer in every respect

...Performs all duties without prompting

...Makes positive, supportable decisions

...Decisive response to any tasking

...Abundance of personal dedication and self-sacrifice

...Epitomizes highest professional standards

...Rare blend of reliability and dedication

...Total dedication ensures success in any tasking

...Promptly executes all orders

...Unblemished record of proven top performance

...Unselfish devotion to duty

…High technical ability

…Sets and achieves high goals

…Comprehensive technical knowledge

…At the forefront of peer group

…Sets and maintains a high standard of performance

…Can always be counted on to get the job done

…Maintains a punishing and productive work schedule

…Unquenchable thirst for knowledge

…Realizes that success requires personal sacrifice

…Always busy and involved in something productive

…Effective in the execution of demanding tasks

…Takes decisive and positive action

…Highly skilled in all facets of technical specialty

…Personal talent rivaled by few

…Demonstrated enthusiasm to any task at hand

…Successfully meets multiple challenges simultaneously

…Productive, admirable results

…Adapts to a new work environment particularly rapid

…Intense dedication and cheerful enthusiasm

…An asset to any organization

…Comprehensive technical knowledge

…Consistently gives quality performance

…job aggressive and a hard charger

The following pages contain bullets/phrases without an ending. This allows the drafter to select an appropriate beginning and add whatever ending is desired.

...Gives wholehearted support to ...

...Achieved impressive results in/by ...

...Top performer. Merits serious consideration for ...

...Displays special skill and knowledge in field of ...

...Did a masterful job in/as ...

...The foremost authority in/on ...

...Without equal in ability to ...

...Preeminent in ability to ...

...A top specialist in the field of ...

...Excels in ability to ...

...Surpasses peers in sheer ability to ...

...Great mental aptitude for ...

...Has full insight and understanding of ...

...Advanced education in skill in/as ...

...Has the knowledge and competence to ...

...Tremendous natural ability to/for ...

...Widely respected for ability to ...

...Furthers technical specialty by ...

...Rejuvenated and put new life into ...

...Transformed below average organization into ...

...Totally involved in successful effort to ...

...Established new standards of excellence in ...

...Performance goes beyond limits of ...

...The leading force and influence in ...

...Actively supports and encourages ...

...Successfully carried out ...

...A strong advocate of ...

...Gives full spirit and support to ...

...Ever energetic, looks forward to ...

...Extremely high degree of excellence in ...

...A perfect example of ...

...Exhibits all essential elements of ...

...Unlimited potential with the capacity to ...

...Made significant progress in/on ...

...An essential ingredient in the highly successful ...

...Routinely receives high praise when ...

...Developed a landmark ...

...Masterful ability to ...

...Enjoys the especially difficult and complex job of ...

...A remarkably skilled ...

...Inexhaustible source of ...

...Firmly established as the top ...

...Routinely prevails over others in/at ...

...Impressive accomplishments include ...

...Extraordinary ability to ...

...Has a natural ability for ...

...Has acquired the necessary attributes to ...

...Praiseworthy characteristics include ...

...An accomplished and proficient ...

...Has substantial knowledge of ...

...Cheerfully devotes off-work time to ...

...Played a vital role in ...

...Assumed the greater responsibilities of ...

...An acknowledged expert in ...

...Uncompromising standards of ...

...Strong leadership resulted in ...

...Totally mastered each and every aspect of ...

...Represents the embodiment of ...

...Spearheaded the highly successful ...

...Simplified and streamlined procedures to/for ...

…Takes exceptional pride in …

…Has a natural gift for …

…Impressively managed the diverse and complex …

…Established strict controls in/on …

…Through acute diligence managed to …

…Routinely hand picked to …

…Produced commendable results in/as …

…Successfully managed a wide range of …

…Instrumental in the successful completion of …

…Personal drive hastened the progress on …

…Stresses the importance of …

…Displays intense dedication in/to …

…Earned high praise and acclaim by/for …

…Can accommodate a wide range of …

…Has special talents for …

…Achieved resounding success in/by …

…Quickly surged ahead of peers in/by …

…Successfully carried out …

…Fully experienced in practical application of …

…Successfully fused together all elements of …

…Skilled in art of …

…Maintains highest standards of …

…The driving force behind …

…Performance routinely exceeds …

…Knows the value of …

…Has a positive, clear view of …

…Creates favorable relationships with …

…Has natural aptitude for …

…Insatiable appetite for …

…Unquenchable quest for knowledge in …

…Prompt and proper in response to …

…Thoroughly understands …

…Provided masterful insight into …

…Became a force in ability to …

…Created perfect foundation for/to …

…Innovative ideas led to …

…Motivating force in achieving significant improvement in …

…Enjoys devising new ways to …

…Foresight and innate sense of leadership led to …

…Use of sound and prudent judgment led to …

…Intense personal drive resulted in …

…Maintains highest standards of …

…Highly specialized in …

…Conforms to exacting standards of …

…Held in high esteem for ability to …

…Possesses requisite competence and aptitude for/to …

…Overwhelming capacity to/for …

…An over abundance of energy and …

…Stands above peers in ability to …

…Succeeded in reaching new heights in …

…Very proficient in/as …

…Especially skilled and adept in/at …

…Maintains a sharp edge in …

…Has decisive advantage over others in ability to …

…Strong spirit and …

…Has extensive knowledge in/on …

…Contributed to vital interests of organization by …

…An absolute master in/at …

…Made marked improvement in …

…Widely recognized for ability to …

…An indispensable member of …

…Personal initiative directly responsible for …

…Has excellent talent for/in …

…Demonstrated creative intelligence and wisdom by …

…Freely spend many off work hours working on …

…Personal efforts were particularly effective in …

…Concise knowledge and clear understanding of …

…One of the most accomplished experts in/on …

…Contributions both substantial and significant in …

…Successfully faced extremely complex …

…Carefully planned and executed a successful …

…Personal example has been a positive influence on …

…Uniquely skilled in/at …

…Personal initiative directly responsible for …

…Has a veracious appetite for …

…Especially effective in executing demanding duties of …

…Put together a complicated and comprehensive …

…Instrumental in promoting many innovative programs in …

…Personal initiative responsible for upgrade in/of …

…Articulate in ability to …

…Successfully completed a complicated …

…Carefully monitored diverse components of …

...Stimulated improved teamwork in ...

...Industrious manner and positive attitude resulted in ...

...A recognized expert in field of ...

...Successfully overcame all obstacles to ...

...Most impressive performer in ...

...Places proper and heavy emphasis in/on ...

...Developed superb plan of action in/on ...

...Earned individual distinction by/for ...

...Rendered outstanding support and service to ...

...Responded positively and correctly to ...

...Technical skill led to early identification and correction of ...

...Superb common sense and professional knowledge led to ...

...Played leading and aggressive role in establishing ...

...Personal energy led to timely completion of ...

...Proved more than equal to the task of ...

...Implemented necessary management concepts that ...

...Met goals across a diverse spectrum by ...

...Won wide acclaim for response to ...

...Demonstrates untiring dedication for/to ...

...Inspires and encourages others by ...

...A quality performer in area of ...

...Has advanced knowledge and skill in ...

...A dominating force in ...

...Takes maximum advantage of opportunities to ...

...Always willing to help others in ...

...A major contributing factor in the success of ...

...Unblemished record of ...

...Technical knowledge and curiosity led to ...

...Does not fall behind when faced with ...

...Has the correct mental approach to ...

...Recently emerged as the best ...

...Personal vision and courage led to ...

...Possesses a wealth of information in/on ...

...Inspires confidence in others by ...

...Superiors had complete confidence in abilities to ...

...Unlimited capacity to/for ...

...Achieved total success in/by ...

...Wins over others with ability to ...

...Quick to grasp the essentials of ...

...Gives others enthusiasm and ability to ...

...Has a natural curiosity for ...

…A person on the move who can readily adjust to …

…Remarkable talent for …

…A champion in the field of …

…Has a fine touch for …

…A dynamic and motivating leader in …

…Ability to organize task and priorities led to …

…Personally molded cohesive and dedicated team of …

…Consistent personal examples of professionalism and …

…Personal initiative and managerial skills overcame …

…Direct personal involvement was instrumental in …

…Unselfishly contributed time and talent to …

…Skillful employment of available manpower resulted in …

…Demonstrated ability that was clearly superior to …

…Professional knowledge significantly improved …

…Established stability and integrity in …

…Consistently met or exceeded demanding duties of …

…Relentless pursuit of excellence paved the way for …

…Instills loyalty and drive in others by …

…Set new standards in/for …

The words in the following section are general usage words. They are action or descriptive words, favorable and unfavorable in nature.

GENERAL USE WORDS

ADJECTIVES

ABLE	ABREAST	ACCEPTABLE
ACCOMMODATING	ACCURATE	ACKNOWLEDGE
ADEQUATE	AGREEABLE	AMBIGUOUS
BENEFICIAL	CAPABLE	CARFREE
CAREFUL	CATEGORICAL	COMPATIBLE
COMPETENT	COMPLAISANT	CONGRUENT
CONSISTENT	CONVENTIAL	CORRECT
CREDIBLE	CURSORY	CUSTOMARY
DEPENDABLE	DEPENDENT	DEVIATE
DOCILE	DRUDGING	DULL
EASYGOING	ECCENTRIC	EFFECTIVE
ELEMENTAL	ELEMENTARY	ENCOURAGING
EQUABLE	EQUITABLE	FACTUAL
FAIR	FAITHFUL	FAVORABLE
FEASIBLE	FELICITOUS	FLEXIBLE
FRAGMENTARY	FUNDAMENTAL	FUZZY
GINGERLY	GOOD	GRADUAL
GUILELESS	HARMLESS	HEEDFUL
HELPFUL	HOPEFUL	HUMBLE
IMPARTIAL	IMPRESSIONABLE	INCLINED
INCONSPICUOUS	INDEFINITE	INDEPENDENT
INDIRECT	INDULGENT	INFORMAL
INFREQUENT	INNOCENT	INTERMITTENT
INVOLUNTARY	INVOLVED	IRONIC

ISOLATED   JUST   LABORIOUS
LEGITIMATE   LENIENT   LIABLE
LOW-KEY   LOW-PRESSURE   LOW-PROFILE

LUKEWARM   MARGINAL   MATTER-OF-COURSE
MATTER-OF-FACT   MEDIOCRE   MERE
METHODICAL   MILD   MODERATE

MODEST   MORAL   NEAT
NEUTRAL   NONCHALANT   NO-NONSENSE
NORMAL   OBEDIENT   OBLIGING

OBSERVANT   ODD   ONE-WAY
ORDERLY   ORDINARY   ORTHODOX
PARTIAL   PASSABLE   PASSIVE

PATIENT   PECULIAR   PERFECTIBLE
PERFUNCTORY   PERTINENT   PLACID
PLIABLE   POTENTIAL   PRACTICAL

PREFFERENTIAL   PREOCCUPIED   PREMATURE
PRESENTABLE   PROPER   PROPITIOUS
PUNCTUAL   PURE   QUALIFIED

QUESTIONABLE   READY   READY-MADE
REALISTIC   REASONABLE   REMEDIAL
RESPONSIVE   RUDIMENTARY   SATISFACTORY

SCRUTABLE   SELF-MADE   SELF-SUFFICIENT
SEMISKILLED   SIMPLE   SLOW
SOPHISTICATED   SPARING   STABLE

STODGY   SUBMISSIVE   SUFFICIENT
SUITABLE   SYSTEMATIC   TEDIOUS
TEMPTING   TOLERABLE   TOLERANT

TRANQUIL   TRIVIAL   UNCOMMON
UNEXCEPTIONAL   UNFAMILIAR   USEFUL
VOLUNTARY   WATCHFUL   WELL-INTENTIONED
WILLING   WILLFUL   WORKABLE
WISHFUL   WOULD-BE

GENERAL USE WORDS

NOUNS

ABILITY
COMMITMENT
COMPLIANCE

AMBIGUITY
COMMONPLACE
COMPOSURE

ATTRIBUTE
COMPETENT
CONCERN

CONFORMANCE
CONJECTURE
DECORUM

CONFORMITY
CREDENTIAL
DEPENDENCE

CONGRUITY
CREDIBILITY
EFFORT

ENIGMA
FELLOWSHIP
FLIP-FLOP

EQUALITY
FIDELITY
FOLLOWER

ETHIC
FIGUREHEAD
FORMALIZE

FRAGMENT
HEARSAY
HEED

GOOD
HUMILITY
IDEALIST

GUIDE
IMITATION
INDIVIDUALIST

INDULGENCE
LABOR
LONER

INTROVERT
LEGITIMACY
MEDIOCRITY

KNACK
LENIENCY
MODERATION

MODESTY
ODDITY
PASSIVISM

MORALIST
ORTHODOXY
PASSIVITY

MORALITY
PARITY
PATIENCE

PLEASANTRY
REALIST
RESISTANCE

PROPENSITY
RELIANCE
RETRIBUTION

PLATITUDE
RESERVE
ROOKIE

RUDIMENT
SCRUPLE
STABILITY

SATISFACTION
SENTIMENT
STAMINA

SCAPEGOAT
SOLITUDE
SURVIVOR

STYLE
TRIVIA

TRANQUILITY
YES-MAN

TREADMILL

GENERAL USE WORDS

VERBS

ABIDE	ACCOMMODATE	AGREE
APPEASE	AVOW	COMPLY
CONFORM	COPE	DABBLE
DEPEND	DEVIATE	DRUDGE
EMPLOY	ENABLE	ENJOY
EXONERATE	FLUCTUATE	GENERALIZE
GUIDE	HOPE	IMITATE
INCLINE	INDOCTRINATE	INTERCEDE
INTERPRET	INTERROGATE	INTROVERT
LABOR	MORALIZE	OBEY
OBLIGE	ORIENTATE	OSCILLATE
PACIFY	PERFORM	PURPOSE
PROPITIATE	PURPORT	QUELL
REGRET	REPUTE	RESERVE
STABILIZE	SUCCEED	SURVIVE
TOLERATE	UNDERSTAND	WANDER

FIXED – LASTING WORDS

ADJECTIVES

ADAMANT	CERTAIN	COHERENT
COHESIVE	DIFFICULT	DURABLE
ENDURABLE	FIRM	FORMIDABLE
HABITUAL	HARD-AND-FAST	HARD-SET
HARD-SHELL	IMMOBILE	IMMOVABLE
IMPENETRABLE	IMPERVIOUS	IMPONDERABLE
INCONTESTABLE		INCONTROVERTIBLE
INCURABLE	INDEFECTIBLE	INDESTRUCTIBLE
INDISPENSABLE	INDISPUTABLE	INESCAPABLE
INEVITABLE	INEXORABLE	INFLEXIBLE
INGRAINED	INIMITABLE	INSUPERABLE
INSURMOUNTABLE	INTRANSIGENT	INVARIABLE
INVINCIBLE	IRREFUTABLE	IRREPRESSIBLE
LASTING	LIMITLESS	LITERAL
LONG-LIVED	PENDURABLE	PREPONDERANT
RENITENT	RESISTANT	RIGID
SOLID	STAUNCH	STEADFAST
STEADY	UNBENDING	UNCOMPROMISING
UNDAUNTED	UNDENIABLE	UNRELENTING

NOUNS

ADHERENCE	CERTAINTY	COHESION
DIFFICULTY	ENDURANCE	PRESISTENCE
RESISTANT		

VERBS

ADHERE	COHERE	ENDLESS
ENDURE	INDURATE	INGRAIN
INUNDATE	PERDURE	PERVADE
RESIST	RIGIDIFY	SOLIDIFY
WITHSTAND		

MORE OR LESS

ABUNDANT (A)	CELING (N)	COLOSSAL (A)
ENORMOUS (A)	EXCESSIVE (A)	FINITE (A)
EXORDITANCE (N)	EXORBITANT (A)	EXTRAVAGENT (A)
FULL-SCALE (A)	GIGANTIC (A)	GOOD DEAL (N)
GOODLY (A)	GREAT (A)	HUGE (A)
IMMEASURABLE (A)	IMMENSE (A)	IMMENSITY (N)
INCALCULABLE (A)	INFINITE (A)	INNUMERABLE (A)
INNUMEROUS (A)	LARGE (A)	LEAST (A)
LESS (A)	LITTLE (A)	MAMMOTH (A)
MAXIMIZE (V)	MAXIMUM (N)	MEAGER (A)
MINIMIZE (V)	MINIMUM (N)	MINISH (V)
MINOR (A)	MINUSCULE (N)	MINUTE (A)
MONUMENTAL (A)	MULTITUDE (N)	MYRIAD (N)
NEGLIGIBLE (A)	NOMINAL (A)	NAUGHT (N)
PALTRY (A)	PAUCITY (N)	SLACKEN (V)
SLACKER (N)	SMALL (A)	SLACKEN (V)
TREMENDOUS (A)	VAST (A)	WANE (A)

Legend: (A) Adjective   (N) Noun   (V) Verb

UNFAVORABLE

REPORTS

UNFAVORABLE REPORTS

The following section contains material that is UNFAVORABLE in nature

The structure, content, and format used to document UNFAVORABLE reports are no different from the FAVORABLE Section.

The UNFAVORABLE words and PHRASES/BULLETS used in this section of the book are more than sufficient to draft UNFAVORABLE reports. As can be seen from the examples on the following pages, describing poor or unfavorable performance is mostly a matter of listing what an individual fails to do, or does not do properly or correctly.

Almost all of the material used in the FAVORABLE Section of this book can be used for UNFAVORABLE comments simply by changing the key FAVORABLE ADJECTIVES, NOUNS, or VERBS to the UNFAVORABLE equivalent.

UNFAVORABLE WRITE-UP - SAMPLE

Name performance, behavior, and attitude took a downward turn at the start of this reporting period and continue to decline. (Name) is intelligent and clever and regardless of the offense or circumstances he has a ready made excuse. His recollections of recent conversations with various superiors routinely turn out to be in complete disagreement with those superiors. Constant vigilance is required to keep him at his work site and gainfully employed. He is a detriment to the morale and good order of (organization). Frequent counseling has been fruitless. (Name) is unreliable, untrustworthy, and is a burden to this organization.

(Name) performance is substandard across the board. He has been reprimanded by the Commanding Officer (...) times for violation of various UCMJ Articles. Routinely questioning the motives of superiors, he asks for an undue amount of justification when assigned tasks. His frequent display of immaturity, bad judgment, and use of half-truths highlight his inability to adjust to a military lifestyle. He gets a haircut only when directed by superiors and routinely fails personnel inspections. Counseling has been required on numerous occasions for lateness, an attitude problem, and a habit of straying from assigned work area. (Name) lack of enthusiasm, constant complaining, and unwillingness to do his share of the work have had a detrimental effect on the morale of (organization).

(Name) overall performance is below standard. He requires close and constant supervision to complete tasks because he is unable to keep his mind on the job at hand. Tardiness and an inability to pass personnel and room inspections also detract from his performance. He has not demonstrated any ability to perform duties independent of supervision and he possesses no leadership qualities. Frequent counseling in all substandard performance areas has not resulted in any significant, lasting improvement. He is immature in behavior and lacks the mental acuity to think through routine daily situations. (Name) is unable to work harmoniously with others and does not promote good morale.

(Name) is a competent performer with average technical skills. His effort and attention to detail during the early part of this reporting period was high. However, his performance, across the board, declined during the middle of this period because of personal problems. He had difficulty reporting on time for duty, concentrating on his work, and in general presenting an acceptable military appearance. Initial counseling sessions failed to lead to any positive results. Additional later counseling did improve his performance. More recently his attitude, behavior, and appearance have improved significantly, and have returned to the same high level displayed early in this reporting period.

143

(Name) is a below average performer. He works diligently to arrive at a satisfactory conclusion of an assigned task. His supervisory skills are lacking as demonstrated by the lackluster performance of his subordinates. Real improvement in his leadership skills are needed before he can be recommended for advancement. Generally a good worker, he sometimes becomes complaisant and requires a reminder to present a more professional attitude and appearance.

UNFAVORABLE – PERSONALITY

ADJECTIVES
The following list of words express, define, state, or describe UNFAVORABLE personality characteristics, traits, performance, or results.

ABERRANT	ABHORRENT	ABRASIVE
ABSENTMINDED	ADOLESCENT	ALOFF
AMBIVALENT	ANTAGONISTIC	ANTISOCIAL
APATHETIC	APPALLING	ARROGANT
ASTRAY	BASHFUL	BELLIGERENT
BERSERK	BLAND	BLUNT
BOISTEROUS	BRASH	BRASSY
CALLOUS	CARELESS	COCKSURE
COCKY	COLD	COLORLESS
COMPLACENT	CONDESCENDING	CONTEMPTIBLE
CORRUPT	CRASS	CRUDE
CRUSTY	CURT	CYNICAL
DECEPTIVE	DEFIANT	DEPRESSED
DERELICT	DESPAIRING	DESPONDENT
DEVIANT	DEVIOUS	DIE-HARD
DIFFIDENT	DISAGREEABLE	DISCOURTEOUS
DISDAINFUL	DISINCLINED	DISLOYAL
DISREPUTABLE	DISSATISFIED	DRABBER

ENERVATE	EGOCENTRIC	EXANIMATE
FACETIOUS	FAITHLESS	FASTIDIOUS
FATUOUS	FAULTFINDING	FECKLESS

FICKLE	FINICKY	FLACCID
FLAPPABLE	FOOLHARDY	FOOLISH
FOPPISH	FORGETFUL	FRACTIOUS

FRUSTRATED	FURIOUS	FUSSY
GALLING	GAUCHE	GARRULOUS
GRUDGING	HALF-BAKED	HALF-COCKED

HALFHEARTED	HAPLESS	HAPPY-GO-LUCKY
HARDHANDED	HARDHEADED	HARD-HEARTED
HARD-NOSED	HEARTLESS	HEAVY-HANDED

HEEDLESS	HIGH-STRUNG	HIGH-TONED
HOSTILE	HUMORLESS	HURTFUL
HYPERCRITICAL	ILLEGIBLE	ILL-HUMORED

ILL-MANNERED	ILL-NATURED	IMMATURE
IMMODERATE	IMMORAL	IMPATIENT
IMPERSONAL	IMPERTINENT	IMPETUOUS

IMPIOUS	IMPOLITE	IMPRUDENT
IMPUDENT	INANE	INAPT
INARTICULATE	INATTENTIVE	INCOGITANT

INCOHERENT	INCOMPETENT	INCONCEIVABLE
INCONGRUOUS	INCONSIDERATE	INDECISIVE
INDIFFERENT	INDIGNANT	INDISCREET

INDOLENT	INELOQUENT	INEPT
INEXPERT	INEXPLICIT	INFIRM
INFURIATE	INHARMONIOUS	INHOSPITABLE

INHUMANE	INIMICAL	INJUDICIOUS
INSENSIBLE	INSENSITIVE	INSINCERE
INSIPID	INSOLENT	INSUBORDINATE

INSURGENT	INVECTIVE	INVIDIOUS
IRATE	IRKSOME	IRRATIONAL
IRRESOLUTE	IRRESPONSIBLE	IRRESPONSIVE
IRRITABLE	JEALOUS	KINDLESS
LACKADAISICAL	LACKLUSTER	LACONIC
LAX	LETHARGIC	LIFELESS
LIGHT-HEADED	LOATH	LOATHSOME
LOQUACIOUS	LOW-MINDED	LOW-SPIRITED
MALADJUSTED	MALEVOLENT	MALICIOUS
MANNERLESS	MEEK	MERCILESS
MISCHEVIOUS	MISTAKEN	MOODY
NAÏVE	NEGLECTFUL	NEVERLESS
OBNOXIOUS	OBSTINATE	OFFENSIVE
OPPRESSIVE	OUTSPOKEN	OVERBEARING
OVERCONFIDENT	PARANOID	PEEVISH
PERMISSIVE	PERTINACIOUS	PESSIMISTIC
PETULANT	PITILESS	POMPUS
PORTENTOUS	PREJUDICIAL	PRUDISH
PRYING	QUARRELSOME	REASONLESS
REBELLIOUS	RELUCTANT	REMISS
REMORSELESS	REPREHENSIBLE	REPROBATE
REPUGNANT	REPULSIVE	RESENTFUL
RHETORICAL	RUDE	RUTHLESS
SARCASTIC	SCORNFUL	SELF-CENTERED
SELF-CONSCIOUS	SELF-DEFEATING	SELF-IMPORTANT
SELFISH	SELFPRIGHTEOUS	SELF-SERVING
SHALLOW	SHAMEFUL	SHAMELESS
SHARP-TONGUED	SHIFTLESS	SHIFTY
SHORTSIGHTED	SHORT-TEMPERED	SMUG
SNIDE	SNUFFY	SOFTHEADED

SORROW	SPIRITLESS	SPITEFUL
SUBTLE	SULLEN	SUPERCILIOUS
SURLY	TACTLESS	TEMPERAMENTAL

TEPID	THANKLESS	THOUGHTLESS
TIMID	TIMOROUS	TROUBLESOME
TURBULENT	UNACCOMPLISHED	UNADVISED

UNAPT	UNCHARITABLE	UNCOMFORTABLE
UNDECIDED	UNDERHANDED	UNFAIR
UNFEELING	UNFIT	UNFRIENDLY

UNGRACIOUS	UNINTERESTING	UNMANNERLY
UNMERCIFUL	UNPLEASANT	UNPOPULAR
UNPRINCIPLED	UNPROFESSIONAL	UNREALISTIC

UNREASONABLE	UNRULY	UNSCRUPULOUS
UNSEASONED	UNSKILLED	UNSKILLFUL
UNSOCIABLE	UNSTABLE	UNSUITABLE

UNTIDY	UNTRUTHFUL	UNWILLING
VAIN	VERBOSE	VINDICTIVE
VIOLENT	WANTON	WEAKHEARTED

WEAK-MINDED	WILL-LESS	WITLESS
WORDY	WRETCH	WRETCHED
WROTH	WRY	

UNFAVORABLE – PERSONALITY

NOUNS

ABERRANT	ABUSE	ALTERCATION
ANTAGONIST	APATHY	ARROGANCE
AUDACITY	BILLIGERENCE	BERSERK

CHAOS	CHARADE	COMPLACENCY
CONDESCENDENCE	CONFLICT	CONTEMPT
CORRUPTION	COVER-UP	DECEPTION

DEFIANCE	DEGRADATION	DERELICTION
DESPONDENCY	DISAGREEMENT	DISCONTENT
DISFAVOR	DISDAIN	DISGUST
DISILLUSION	DISLOYALTY	DISMAY
DISREPUTE	DISRESPECT	DISSENSION
DISSENT	DISSENTER	DURESS
EGOISM	EGOTISM	ENMITY
FAKE	FALSITY	FATIGUE
FAULTFINDING	FAVORITISM	FEUD
FLEDGLING	FLUSTER	FOIBLE
FOLLY	FOOLISHNESS	FOOT-DRAGGING
FOUL-UP	FRACAS	FRAUD
FRUSTRATION	FUROR	FURY
GALL	GARRULITY	GRIEVANCE
GRIMACE	GRUDGE	GUISE
HALF-TRUTH	HATRED	HOSTILITY
ILLITERACY	ILLOGIC	IMPATIENCE
IMPERTINENCE	IMPROPRIETY	IMPRUDENCE
IMPUDENCE	INABILITY	INACCURACY
INAPTITUDE	INCAPACITY	INCERTITUDE
INCOMPATIBILITY	INCOMPETENCE	INDECISION
INDIFFERENCE	INDIGNATION	INDIGNITY
INDISCIPLINE	INDISCRETION	INEPTITUDE
INEQUALITY	INEQUITY	INEXPERIENCE
INGRATITUDE	INHARMONY	INIQUITY
INJUSTICE	INSOLENCE	INSTABILITY
INSULT	INTOLERANCE	IRE
JEALOUSY	KNOW-IT-ALL	LAXITY
LETHARGY	LOATHING	MALEVOLENCE
MALICE	NONCONFORMIST	MENACE

MISGIVING	MISUNDERSTANDING	NEGLIGENCE
OBSESSION	OUTBURST	OUTRAGE
PANIC	PARTISAN	PESSIMISM
POMPOSITY	PREJUDICE	PRUDE
QUITTER	RAGE	RAMPAGE
REBUFF	REFUSAL	RELUCTANCE
REMORSE	REPRESSION	REPRIMAND
REPROACH	REPUGNANCE	REPULSION
RESENTMENT	RHETORIC	RHETORICIAN
RIDICULE	RIVALRY	SARCASM
SCOFF	SCORN	SELF-CONCEIT
SELF-DOUBT	SELF-INTEREST	SHAM
SKIRMISH	SPITE	STUPOR
STYMIE	TEDIUM	TEMERITY
TROUBLEMAKER	TRUANT	TURMOIL
UNREASON	UNTRUTH	WEAKNESS
WRONGDOER	WRONGDOING	

UNFAVORABLE – PERSONALITY

VERBS

ABUSE	ACCOST	ANTAGONIZE
APPALL	BAFFLE	BELITTLE
BERATE	BETRAY	BIAS
BLUNDER	CENSURE	CHASTISE
COERCE	CONDEMN	CONFUSE
CONSPIRE	CRITICIZE	DEGRADE
DEMEAN	DEMORALIZE	DEPRESS
DESPAIR	DESPOND	DISACCORD
DISAGREE	DISCORD	DISDAIN

DISGRUNTLE	DISGUST	DISMAY
DISPUTE	DISREGARD	DISRESPECT
DISSATISFY	DISSENT	EMBITTER
ENRAGE	FALSIFY	FINAGLE
FLAUNT	FLOUT	FORESTALL
FORFEIT	FORGET	FRET
FRUSTRATE	FUMBLE	GRIEVE
GRIPE	HARASS	HUMILIATE
IGNORE	IMPERSONALIZE	INFLAME
INFRINGE	INSULT	INTERFERE
INTERRUPT	INTIMIDATE	INTRUDE
IRK	LOATHE	MALINGER
MEDDLE	MISAPPLY	MISAPPROPRIATE
MISBECOME	MISBEHAVE	MISCALCULATE
MISCONDUCT	MISCONSTRUE	MISFIT
MISGUIDED	MISINTERPRET	MISJUDGE
MISLEAD	MISMANAGE	MISUNDERSTANDING
MISUSE	MUDDLE	OFFEND
OPPOSE	OPPRESS	OSTRACIZE
OVEREXTEND	OVERRACT	OVERSIMPLIFY
PATRONIZE	PERSECUTE	PERTURB
PLOD	PROCRASTINATE	PRY
RELAPSE	RELENT	RENOUNCE
REPREHEND	REPRESS	REPROBATE
REPUDIATE	REPULSE	RESENT
SCORN	SHIRK	SQUABBLE
STUPEFY	STYMIED	SUCCUMB
UNDERMINE	UNNERVE	WANGLE

UNFAVORABLE

The following list of words express, define, state, or describe UNFAVORABLE individual intellect, intelligence, knowledge, wisdom, or reasoning

ADJECTIVES

ABSURD	CRASS	DENSE
DULL	FOOLISH	IGNORANT
ILLITERATE	ILLOGICAL	INANE
INCONSEQUENT	INEPT	INSENSIBLE
INSIGNIFICANT	IRRATIONAL	MEANINGLESS
MINDLESS	ORDINARY	RIDICULOUS
SENSELESS	SHALLOW	SHORTSIGHTED
SIMPLE	SIMPLE-MINDED	SUPERFICIAL
TRIFLING	UNACQUAINTED	UNAWARE
UNCONVERSANT	UNDISCERNING	UNDISTINGUISHED
UNFAMILIAR	UNIMAGINATIVE	UNINFORMATIVE
UNINFORMED	UNINTELLIGENT	UNKNOWING
UNKNOWN	UNLEARNED	UNLETTERED
UNPERCEPTIVE	UNREASONING	UNREFINED
UNSCHOLARLY	UNTAUGHT	UNTUTORED
UNVERSED	UNWISE	

NOUNS

DULLNESS	IGNORANCE	INCAPACITY
INEPTITUDE	INSENSIBILITY	IRRATIONALITY
SENILE	SENILITY	SHALLOWNESS
SHORTSIGHTEDNESS		STUPIDITY
SUPERFICIALITY	UNKNOWING	UNWITTINGNESS

NEGATIVE – SHORTCOMING WORDS

The following list of words express, define, state, or describe UNFAVORABLE characteristics, traits, performance, or results not solely individual or personal.

ADJECTIVES

ABNORMAL	ABRUPT	ADVERSE
AMISS	ASKEW	AWRY
CONFLICTING	COSTIVE	CUMBERSOME
DEFECTIVE	DEFICIENT	DESPERATE
DISAPPOINTING	DISPASSIONATE	DISRUPTIVE
DETRIMENTAL	DUBIOUS	EFFETE
EFFORTLESS	ELUSIVE	EQUIVOCAL
EROSIVE	ERRANT	ERRATIC
EVASIVE	ERRONEOUS	FACILE
FALSE	FARCICAL	FARFETCHED
FLAGRANT	FLIMSY	FORMLESS
FRAGILE	FRAIL	FRAUDULENT
FRIVOLOUS	FRUITLESS	FUTILE
GLOOMY	GLUM	GRAVE
GREVIOUS	GRIM	GROSS
HAPHAZARD	HARD PUT	HARSH
HELPLESS	HERKY-JERKY	HIT-OR-MISS
HOPELESS	HORRENDOUS	HUMDRUM
HUMILIATING	IDLE	ILL-ADVISED
ILLAUDIBLE	ILLEGAL	ILL-FATED
ILL-GOTTEN	ILLICIT	IMAGINATIVE
IMAGINARY	IMPERFECT	IMPOSSIBLE
IMPOTENT	IMPRACTICABLE	IMPRACTICAL
IMPROBABLE	IMPROPER	INACCURATE

INACTIVE	INADEQUATE	INADVISABLE
INAPPROPRIATE	INCAPABLE	INCOMPARABLE
INCOMPATIBLE	INCOMPLETE	INCONSEQUENTIAL
INCONSIDERABLE	INCONSISTENT	INCONVENIENT
INCORRECT	INCORRIGIBLE	INDEFENSIBLE
INDEFINABLE	INDISCERNIBLE	INDISTINCT
INEFFECTIVE	INEFFECTUAL	INEFFICIENT
INELIGIBLE	INEXACT	INEXCUSABLE
INEXPLICABLE	INFERIOR	INOPPORTUNE
INSECURE	INSIDIOUS	INSIGNIFICANT
INSUBSTANTIAL	INSUFFERABLE	INSUFFICIENT
INSUPPORTABLE	INTOLERABLE	INTOLERANT
INTRACTABLE	INTRUSIVE	INVALID
IRREDEEMABLE	IRREGULAR	IRRELATIVE
IRRELEVANT	LAST	LIMITED
LOST	LOW-GRADE	LOW-LEVEL
LUDICROUS	MALADROIT	MEANINGLESS
MISERABLE	MUNDANE	NEGATIVE
NEGLIGENT	NONPRODUCTIVE	NULL
OBSCURE	OBSOLETE	OUTCAST
OUTLANDISH	OUT-OF-DATE	OUTRAGEOUS
OVERDUE	PATHETIC	PETTY
PRECARIOUS	PREPOSTEROUS	PROBLEM
PURPOSELESS	REDUNDANT	RESISTLESS
RUN-DOWN	RUSTY	SCANT
SCANTY	SHABBY	SHAKY
SKEPTICAL	SLIPSHOD	SLOPPY
SMALL-SCALE	SORROWFUL	SPARSE
SPORADIC	SPOTTY	STAGNANT
SUBNORMAL	SUBSTANDARD	SUPERFICIAL
SUPERFLUOUS	THRIFTLESS	TIRESOME

TRICKY	TRITE	UNCERTAIN
UNEASY	UNFAVORABLE	UNFORTUNATE
UNLAWFUL	UNORGANIZED	UNSETTLED
UNSUCCESSFUL	UNTRUE	UNWORTHY
USELESS	VALUELESS	WANTING
WASHED-UP	WASTED	WASTEFUL
WEAK	WEARIFUL	WEARISOME
WEARY	WHIMSICAL	WISHY-WASHY
WORSE	WORST	WORTHLESS
WRONG	WRONGFUL	

NOUNS

ADVERSITY	BLEMISH	CHAGRIN
CONFUSION	DEFECT	DEMERIT
DEMISE	DEPENDENCY	DETRIMENT
DEVIATE	DISADVANTAGE	DISAPPOINTMENT
DISASTER	DISCORD	DISCREDIT
DISORDER	DISPARITY	EBB
EGOIST	ENCUMBRANCE	ERROR
EXCUSE	EYESORE	FAILURE
FAULT	FIASCO	FIZZLE
FLAW	FLUTTER	FORFEIT
FRICTION	FUTILITY	GLITCH
HAPHAZARD	HARDSHIP	HARM
HINDRANCE	IMBALANCE	IMPARITY
IMPERFECTION	IMPOSSIBILITY	INACTION
INADEQUACY	INATTENTION	INCONSISTENCY
INCONSONANCE	INCONVENIENCE	INEFFICIENCY
INFRACTION	INSIGNIFICANCE	INTERFERENCE
INTRUSION	INVALIDITY	IRREGULARITY

LACK	LAG	LAPSE
LIABILITY	LOSER	MEANDER
MISFORTUNE	MISHAP	MIX-UP
NONSENSE	NUISANCE	OVERSIGHT
PELL-MELL	PITFALL	PROBLEM
QUIBBLE	REGRESS	REGRESSION
SHODDY	SHORTCOMING	SHORTFALL
SLOPWORK	TENSION	TRAVESTY
UNCERTAINTY	WASTE	

VERBS

COLLAPSE	CONCEAL	CONCEDE
CONDESCEND	CRIMP	DEBASE
DENOUNCE	DEPRIVE	DESTROY
DETERIORATE	DILUTE	DIMINISH
DISAPPOINT	DISRUPT	DISTORT
DODGE	DWINDLE	EBB
ELUDE	ENCUMBER	ERODE
EXACERBATE	FADE	FAIL
FAKE	FALTER	FLOP
FLOUNDER	FLUNK	FOIL
FOUNDER	GLOOM	HAMPER
HARM	HINDER	IMMOBILIZE
IMPAIR	IMPEDE	INCAPACITATE
IRRITATE	LACK	LAG
LAPSE	LESSEN	LIMP
LOWER	MAR	MISTAKE
NEGATE	NEGLECT	OBSTRUCT
OUTS	QUIT	REFUSE
REJECT	RELINQUISH	RETARD
SUPPRESS	TRANSGRESS	VIOLATE
WEAKEN	WILT	WORSEN

BULLET PHRASES – UNFAVORABLE

...Inexcusable behavior

...Inconsiderate and uncaring

...Dull, uninspiring leader

...Indolent, sluggish personality

...Not an effective leader

...Illogical performance

...Produces inaccurate results

...Causes disorder and unrest

...Lacking in knowledge

...Has defeatist attitude

...Weak, ineffective leader

...Shows little or no effort

...Erodes morale and team spirit

...Inferior workmanship

...Flagrant violation of orders

...Disagreeable personality

...Causes gloom in others

...Overly bold and assertive

...Not fit

...Of little value

...Distasteful behavior

...Inappropriate actions

...Not manageable

...Slow to act

...Abnormal behavior

...Abrupt manner

...Faulty work

...Dispassionate leader

...Erratic work habits

...Weak and inadequate

...Not well organized

...Lacks physical vigor

...Indecisive and evasive

...Non-productive worker

...Lacks charisma

...Attracts trouble

...Ambiguous and evasive

...Crude, course personality

...Operates in a vacuum

...Poor planner, great hindsight

...Vague and ambiguous

...Careless work habits

...Professionally stagnant

...Disagreeable personality

...Arrogant, overbearing manner

...Crude, tactless manner

...Abrupt, tactless manner

...Fails to observe regulations

...Spiritless, lifeless leader

...Unable to master job

...Careless in manner and action

...Unprincipled behavior

...Overbearing and oppressive

...Careless, untidy appearance

...Ill-humored personality

...Accepts orders reluctantly

...Undisciplined and unruly

...Stubborn and obstinate

...Aberrant behavior

...Unstable personality

...Impersonal leader

...Inferior performance

...Evasive and indirect

...Emotionally immature

...Adolescent behavior

...Overly talkative

...Antisocial behavior

...Deviant behavior

...Drab, dull personality

...Acts on impulse

...Unfriendly disposition

...Fails to plan ahead

...Indecisive leader

...Distorts the truth

...Abusive language

...Obstinate and impudent

...Fault-finding to excess

...Misuses position

...Vain, self-centered personality

...Reluctant, unwilling performer

...Temperamental behavior

...Tends to be troublesome

...Maladjusted personality

...Bad in manner and disposition

...Indiscreet and thoughtless action

...Lax in performance and behavior

...Impolite and unmannerly

...Short-tempered and arrogant

...Prone to indecisiveness

...Weak, vacillating leadership

...Prankish, childish mannerism

...Impolite, insulting manner

...Insincere, careless leader

...Disrespectful to superiors

...Cold, indifferent attitude

...Corrupt, immoral character

...Argumentative toward others

...Threat to good morale

...Disorderly conduct

...Undignified manner

...Provokes arguments

...Careless appearance

...Failed to improve

...A problem personality

...Unpredictable behavior

...Loses control

...Totally unconcerned

...Lack of desire

...Aggressive attitude

...Completely helpless

...Impedes progress

...Devious and cunning

...Low self-esteem

...Lack of confidence

...Ignores reality

...Boisterous behavior

...Rude personality

...Shirks responsibility

...Mentally malnourished

...Misrepresents the facts

...Interferes with progress

...Leadership vacuum

...Easily excitable and troublesome

...Improper behavior and conduct

...Indifferent towards others

...Seriously endangers morale

...Uncaring towards others

...Impervious to counseling

...Carefree attitude and work

...Subject to daily failure

...Ignores advice of others

...Inflexible, rigid taskmaster

...Practices deceit and trickery

...Fabricates the truth

...Undesirable personality traits

...Unsound management practices

...Corruptive, dishonest nature

...Irritates and annoys others

...Mundane leadership skills

...Ineffectual skills

...Emotionally immature

...Mistaken judgment

...A complainer

...Bad judgment

...Difficult to reason with

...Incapable and inept

...Distant and impersonal

...Abrasive personality

...Plots and schemes

...Throws weight around

...Creates resentment

...Slow to act

...Wasted opportunities

...Incites arguments

...Insensitive leadership

...Short tempered

...Inhibits progress

...Shuns duties

...Unimpressive leader

...Faulty workmanship

...Deviates from standards

...Discourages team unity

...Contemptible and arrogant

...Avoids work and responsibility

...Suppresses subordinate initiative

...Circumvents chain of command

...Loses emotional control

...Meager productiveness

...Becomes emotionally violent

...Serious errors in judgment

...Lacks proper mental discipline

...Becomes easily frustrated

...Innate aversion to work

...Imperceptible progress

...Not dependable or reliable

...Unpredictable work habits

...Consistent poor performance

...Complete disregard for authority

...Does no more than required

...Less than moderate success

...Unjustly exploits others

...Meek manner

...Brash and immature

...Incompetent manager

...Without compassion

...Blatant negligence

...Disruptive influence

...Abnormal behavior

...Argues to excess

...Mediocre abilities

...Mild learning disability

...Common and ordinary

...Inflexible leader

...Dull, trite personality

...Undermines morale

...Constantly complains

...Lack of initiative

...Negative attitude

...Open discontent?

...Quarrelsome nature

...Arrogant and overbearing

...Finds excessive leisure time

...Unable to control emotions

...Intentionally avoids work

...Deliberately refuses work

...Lack of pride in work

...Aggressive temperament

...Lacks depth and substance

...Unwilling to obey orders

...Without sorrow or remorse

...Immaturity and bad judgment

...Behavior and attitude problems

...Unimpressive performance

...Prejudicial to good order

...Detrimental to team spirit

...Less than marginal performer

...Fails to monitor subordinates

...Causes extra work for others

...Reluctant to abide by rules

...Continuing discipline problem

...Exercises bad judgment

...Unacceptable behavior

...Ignores direction

...Flouts authority

...Not job-aggressive

...Lags behind others

...Stirs up trouble

...Becomes easily excited

...Breaks down morale

...Lacks persistence

...Acts on impulse

...Not trustworthy

...Not reliable

...Weak personality

...Abrupt manner

...Apathetic leader

...Creates problems

...Lackadaisical attitude

...Plagued by indecision

...Frequent complainer

...Unwilling to conform

...Irregular work habits

...Unable to stay abreast of job

...Interferes with progress

...Indecisive under pressure

...Lacks self-discipline

...Hot tempered and easily angered

...Explosive disposition

...Obvious lack of motivation

...Shirks responsibility

...Not an inspiring leader

...Lack of initiative

...Disobedient and disrespectful

...Indecisive leader

...Doubtful and confusing leadership

...Indecisive in action

...Concerned with own self-interest

...Aimless leadership

...Disagreeable personality

...Inattentive to detail

...Openly disagrees with superiors

...Emotional difficulty

...Fails to accomplish tasks

...Irrational behavior

...Negative outlook and attitude

...Inconsistent worker

...Asks undue questions

...Erodes good order

...Lax in carrying out duties

...Prone to argument

...Requires routine reminders

...A slacker

...Wears down team spirit
...Slow, plodding worker

...Abrasive personality
...Weak leader

...Questionable leadership practices

...Impersonal, detached leader

...Gets less than desired results

...Not receptive to counseling

...Frequent bad judgment

...Marginal performer at best

...overly aggressive personality

...Exerts minimum effort

...Verbally abuses others

...No future potential or value

...Spreads ill-will and disharmony

...Overly bold and brash

...Careless attention to duty

...Non-forgiving leadership traits

...Lack of personal conviction

...Suppresses subordinate growth

...Unable to perform routine tasks

...Abusive and offensive language

...Lacks knowledge and ability

...Manipulates others to own end

...Ingrained disrespectful nature

...Gives misguided direction

...Of little worth or value

...Fails to achieve consistency

…Lack of confidence in abilities

…Helpless without supervision

…A burden to leadership

…Unable to deal with reality

…Disobedient and belligerent

…Needs continued reminders

…Interprets rules loosely

…Improper counseling techniques

…Overbearing and intolerant

…Not firm with subordinates

…Spreads discontent and resentment

…Reluctant to accept direction

…Tries hard, accomplishes little

…Chronic financial problems

…Fails to respond to direction

…Frequently in discord with superiors

…Lacks consistency of performance

…Inflexible, unimaginative leadership

…Instigates and provokes disharmony

…Becomes easily agitated and excited

…Mechanical, non-inventive leadership skills

…Blames others for own shortcomings

…Oppressive in character and action

…Unpleasant appearance and personality

…Deficient in skill and knowledge

…Unable to overcome minor problems

…Unpredictable attention to duty

…Incapable manager and supervisor

…Incapable of sustained satisfactory performance

…Not a potent, effective leader

…Incapable of handling daily duties

…Makes decisions that are not sensible or prudent

…Incompetent without direct, constant supervision

…Unfair and inequitable treatment of subordinates

…Not correct or precise in detail

…Unmanageable off-duty activities

…Behavior is incompatible with good order and discipline

…Failed to live up to expectations

…Disruptive to teamwork and good discipline

…Uncertain and doubtful in making decisions

…Aimless, errant decision making facilities

…Lacks personal sincerity and believability

...Frequently makes false or untrue statements

…Inclined to stray from the truth

…Organization lacks order and cohesiveness

…Self-indulgent, irresponsible leadership

…Impatient with subordinates

…Achieves less than moderately successful results

…Can achieve good results only under no-stress conditions

…Deliberately goes out of way to irritate others

…Intentionally makes minor mistakes

…Efforts frequently prove fruitless and unsuccessful

…Shows little forethought or preparation of task at hand

…Lacks good judgment and common sense

…Insolent, overbearing behavior

…Does not demonstrate a sense of responsibility

…Lackluster and lackadaisical attitude

…Unwilling to listen to reason or fact

…Too submissive and mild mannered to be an effective leader

…Subject to mood changes without warning

…Overreacts to minor incidents

…Criticizes and reprimands subordinates in public

…Blames own shortcomings on others

…Evades and shrinks duty when possible

…Acts out of emotion, not reason

…Becomes easily confused and frustrated

…A complete disappointment

…Makes mistakes through lack of attention

…Argumentative with irritating persistence

…Intentional disregard for following orders

…Excessively lenient in handling subordinates

…Insulting and arrogant personality

…Policies are not uniform or consistent

…Conveniently misunderstands or misinterprets orders

…Difficult to support independent decisions

…Excessively forceful toward subordinates

…Fails to act according to professional standards

…A bad leader and a worse follower

…Plans lack sufficient planning or substance

…Low level of self-confidence

…Habitually reports late

…Lax and careless in performing duties

…Off-duty conduct is disgraceful and unacceptable

…Conduct is beyond bounds of decency

…Frequently breaks rules and disobeys orders

…Overly strict and harsh leadership practices

…Considers work below personal dignity

…Apprehensive about accepting any new challenge

…Does not abide by rules

…Professional development lags behind peers

…Ignores direction and guidance of superiors

…Wasteful and extravagant use of resources

…Alters facts to suit own self-interest

…Strays from work area if not closely watched

…Unable to stay mentally involved with work

…Becomes preoccupied with personal matters

…Deviates sharply from behavioral standards

…Belligerent and hostile personality

…Displays open contempt for authority

…Devoid of hope for improvement

…Has more than a mild dislike for work

…Violates acceptable standards of conduct

...Will violate any rule or regulation not to personal liking

...Written products are not clear or coherent

...Verbally insulting and abusive toward others

...Overly harsh and critical of subordinates

...Blunt and rude in speech and manner

...Unable to choose correct courses of action

...Thoughtless in considering feelings of others

...Insensitive and callous leadership

...Not responsive to guidance or direction

...Destructive to good order and team work

...Unsophisticated behavior and attitude

...Performance highlighted by neglect and indifference

...Unpleasant, objectionable personality

...Unyielding to reason or rationale

...Not a strong leader

...Lacks necessary personal traits to be a good leader

...Exaggerated self-opinion and self-importance

...Acts without giving due consideration to others

...Personal problems demand excessive time and energy

...Neglectful and forgetful work habits

...Lacking in social grace and courtesy

...Will not work unless prompted or prodded

...Lacks orderly mental continuity

...Careless of the feelings of others

...Indiscreet personal affairs

...Unable to restrain or control personal emotions

...Stubbornly opposes corrective counseling

...Refuses to yield or relent to change

...Does not objectively evaluate options

...Leadership style too tolerant and permissive

...Excessive minor infractions of discipline and regulations

...Gross deviation from regulations

...Becomes bogged down in petty, insignificant details

...Shirks duty when possible

...Administrative and disciplinary burden

...Exhibits lack of desire to conform to expected standards

...Persistent minor disciplinary infractions

...Performance a deterrent to good order and discipline

...A liability to the command

...Shows no desire for improvement

...Frequently deviates from established guidelines

...Disrespectful attitude and behavior

...Behavior goes beyond the bounds of good taste

...Exhibits only short periods of success

...Without personal restraint

...Not straightforward and open in manner

...Unable to distinguish right from wrong

...Actions are open to question

...Expects success using guesswork

...Passive and submissive in nature

...Unable to overcome personal problems

...Fails to maintain harmony or cohesiveness

...Work marked by utter, complete failure

...Has personality clashes with others

...Makes careless, avoidable mistakes

...Fails to achieve minimum acceptable standards

...Work frequently falls short of abilities

...Failed to live up to expectations

...Twists recollection of events to own ends

...Performance falls well short of abilities

...Does not have necessary tact and maturity needed

...Very difficult for others to work with

...Incapable of compassionate leadership

...Neglects personal welfare of subordinates

...Evasive when confronted with shortcomings

...Helpless in meeting new situations

...Becomes easily hesitant and confused

...Suitable only for routine, ordinary tasks

...Excuses offered more frequently than good performance

...Tries very hard but achieves little

...Deceptive and deceitful character

...Non-inventive or inspiring leadership

...Exerts undue influence and pressure on subordinates

...Works hard only when personally convenient

...Turns simple tasks into complex problems

...Disagreeing personality has taken a toll on morale

...Agitates others and creates ill-will and discontent

...Routinely questions superiors

...Superficial work does not hold up to close examination

...Overly demanding and self-assertive

...Overly concerned with self-image

...Not a compassionate, caring leader

...Work suffers from plainness and simplicity

...A prankster, not serious minded

...Out of kilter, does not function properly

...Unsuccessful in trying situations

...Discussions frequently turn into heated debates

...Gives in to pressure during crisis situations

...Opposes improvement efforts of others

...Inability to adapt to changing situations

...Unable to stay abreast of changing situations

...Does no more than absolutely necessary

...Willful disobedience of orders

...Open disrespect for authority

...Cannot make proper response under pressure

...Dodges work and responsibility at every opportunity

...Behavior is substandard

...Not job-aggressive

...Waits for things to happen before taking action

...Displays unacceptable behavior and performance

...Relies too heavily on efforts of others

...Below average performer

…Not overly seriously concerned in doing tasks correctly

…Well below level of performance expected

…Manipulates people to meet own ends

…Not prudent in personal financial matters

…Carefree and reckless attitude

…Prejudicial to good order and discipline

…Substandard performance routinely displayed

…Does not get work done in a timely manner

…Attempts to walk a fine line between right and wrong

…Needs continued reminders about personal appearance

…Routinely fails personnel inspections

…Good judgment sometimes impaired by short temper

…Has difficulty getting along with others

…Unwilling to conform to expected standards

…Does not always get all the facts before acting

…Sometimes absent minded or preoccupied

…Interprets rules loosely to own benefit

…Too easily influenced by subordinates

…Becomes withdrawn when confronted on shortcomings

…Degrades or humiliates others

…Deviates from work standards if not closely watched

...Overbearing personality

...Intolerant of any mistakes by others

...Not a strong leadership personality

...Erodes discipline and teamwork

...Abnormally high reluctance to accept routine direction

...Opposes all views other than own

...Not capable of satisfactory performance

...Not firm and resolute with subordinates

...Abrasive personality with an abrupt manner

...Treatment of others less than desired or expected

...Wears down spirit of subordinates

...Behavior subject to sudden bursts of anger

...Inattentive to routine work procedures

...Lacks persistence and patience

...Arbitrarily enforces rules and standards

...Believes job should be subordinate to personal interests

...Unforeseen problems routinely arise

...Gives undue consideration to personal desires

...Accommodating to subordinates to a fault

...Uncompromising stand in even minor matters

...Speaks and acts on impulse

...Does not always think through problem situations

...Overly challenging and aggressive personality

...Blames others for own shortcomings

...Condemns or shuns ideas of others

...Cannot be relied upon to take timely action

...Unconventional leadership produces less than desire results

...Not receptive to constructive counseling

...Views standing orders to own liking

...Irrational and erratic behavior

...Harsh and course in leadership and language

...Can perform only routine tasks correctly

...Subordinates suffer from lack of direction

...Language and treatment are major leadership flaws

...Fails to abide by rules and regulations

...Lacks quality and depth of character

...Gets into verbal confrontation with others

...Leadership lacks direction and purpose

...Rigid thinking restricts future growth

...Unable to cope with difficult situations

...Improper leadership attitude

...Plagued by lack of self-confidence

...Defeatist attitude is a major disappointment

...Ingrained disregard for authority

...Leadership style leaves much to be desired

...Non-forgiving leader

...Asks for an undue amount of justification from seniors

...Exerts only minimum amount of initiative

...Fails to properly supervise subordinates

...Assigns work but does not follow up on progress

...Has difficulty managing paperwork

...Unable to ensure quality work completed in timely manner

...Not steadfast in job commitment

...Leadership ability is questionable at best

...Subordinates are routinely confused about what to do

...Inattentive to detail

...Becomes easily distracted

...Routinely questions superiors

...Reliability oscillates between high and low

...Superiors waste much time counseling substandard work

...Good at jobs that are routine and repetitive in nature

…Has difficulty following direction

…A noticeable decline in performance

…Plagued by indecisiveness

…Has neither the desire nor ability to perform satisfactorily

…Does not always consider the gravity of situation at hand

…Tries hard, accomplishes little

…Frequently overlooks routine but necessary details

…Slow and deliberate work pace

…Does not perform well under stress or pressure

…Usually in compliance with rules and regulations

…Subject to periods of disobedience

…Counseling routinely required for sloppy work

…Does not pay attention to detail

…Performance of duty, across the board, unsatisfactory

…Requires constant supervision

…Often leaves work space without permission

…Less than a positive attitude

…Marginal and inconsistent work

…Reluctant to accept any responsibility

…Work marked by inconsistency and incompleteness

…Sporadic in carrying out instructions

…Frequently displays immaturity and bad judgment

…Inability to meet expected standards

…No a self-starter

…Demonstrates little initiative

…No desire for self improvement

…Received counseling on numerous occasions

…Lack of motivation and initiative

…Acceptance of orders depends upon issuing superior

…Late for work on numerous occasions

…Fails to respond to repeated counseling

…Counseling results in only short-time improvement

…Consistently demonstrated substandard performance

…Shoddy workmanship

…Does not take pride in work or job accomplishment

…Performance is unsatisfactory

…Personal conduct prejudicial to good order and discipline

…Performance is all valleys and no peaks

…Impulsive, acts without due thought or consideration

…Unreliable performance despite counseling

…Negative attitude reflected in marginal performance

…Conduct has degenerated to unacceptable level

…Flagrant violation of direction

…Low level of performance and conduct

…Displays open discontent toward superiors

…Inconsistent in accepting direction

…Performance well below that of peers

…Lets serious matters slip without needed attention

…Less than marginal performer

…Requires almost constant supervision

…Ignores explicit direction of superiors

…Frequently voices displeasure at job assignments

…Not aggressive in meeting established standards

…Migrates between acceptable and unsatisfactory work

…Habitually flouts authority

…Engenders disrespect among peers

…Fails to properly monitor work of subordinates

…Continually commits minor offenses

…Below average performer

…Unresponsive to normal and special counseling

…Generally performs to full potential, but not always

…Disruptive to good order and morale

...Seriously lacking in initiative

...Constant supervision required to complete tasks

...Openly voices disagreement with superiors

...Obvious lack of motivation

...Flouts authority despite numerous counseling attempts

...Unsatisfactory performance in technical specialty

   Lackadaisical attitude toward superiors and job

...Becomes withdrawn when confronted with deficiencies

...Wanders from work space to attend to personal matters

...Negative outlook and disposition

...Openly complains about job assignments

...A burden to superiors

...Inability to comply with simplest direction

...Lacks requisite skill and knowledge to do good work

...Unable to control diverse operations

...Inconsistent performance

...Usually a good worker, but requires routine supervision

...Works without supervision only when the mood strikes

...Total lack of enthusiasm

...Subject to constant complaining

…Unwilling to do fair share of work

…Attitude detrimental to good morale

…Has difficulty following simple orders or direction

…A marginal performer at best

…Must be under constant supervision to complete tasking

…Requires constant reminding to complete jobs on schedule

…Requires direct guidance and supervision

…Immature and undisciplined

…No potential for future useful service

…Reluctant to conform to standards of conduct

…Continuous poor attitude and work performance

…Prolonged decline in performance

…Consistently fails to take action on pending projects

…Numerous shortcomings despite counseling sessions

…Usually gives only half-effort

…Indecisive and undisciplined leadership

…Inability to gain proficiency in technical specialty

…Insufficient motivation to overcome personal deficiencies

...Unable to take constructive criticism and private counseling

…Will not acknowledge mistakes or failures

…Blames others for own shortcomings

…No knack for making positive things happen

…Performance well below expected standards

…Attempts to correct deficiencies have been in vain

…Inappropriate behavior and performance

…Lacks mental depth to comprehend technical matters

…Fabricates the truth

…Slow to learn and develop professionally

The following pages contain bullets/phrases without an ending. This allows you to select an appropriate ending as desired or appropriate.

…Unwilling to put forth necessary effort to …

…Does not give required importance to …

…Habitually gets into trouble by …

…Does not have the ability to …

…Not mentally capable of …

…Below normal level of skill in/as …

…Conduct not fit or becoming of a/an …

…Impairs morale by …

…Unable to maintain a stable balance of …

…Lacks necessary ability to …

183

…Not qualified to be …

…Not worthy of …

…Becomes hostile when approached about …

…Lacking in ability to …

…Of little value in/when …

…Despite counseling and supervision, continues to …

…Overall performance declined because …

…Is of little or no use in/when …

…Failed to achieve consistence in …

…Involved in unethical practice of …

…Behavior not conducive to …

…Unforgiving nature causes …

…Lacks mental courage and conviction to …

…Did not exercise sound judgment by/when …

…Shows apathy and indifference to/toward …

…Blatant disregard for …

…Openly defies and challenges …

…Disenchanted with present duties because …

…Enjoys a low reputation due to …

…Will not maintain commitment to …

...Lacks vigor or patience to ...

...Loses composure when ...

...Rude and impolite when ...

...Slow to learn and develop as a/an ...

...Lacks mental aptitude to ...

...Performance has deteriorated to point of ...

...Not mature enough to ...

...Has not adjusted well to ...

...A misfit, not suited to/for ...

...Lacks the capacity to ...

...Becomes agitated and upset when ...

...Unable to refrain from ...

...Bad habits include ...

...Becomes confused and puzzled when ...

...Upsets normal operations by ...

...Does not satisfy minimum requirements of/for ...

...Does not possess the mental vigor and vitality to ...

...Contemptuous disregard for ...

...Comes under undue emotional strain when ...

...Has open contempt for ...

...Hinders progress by ...

…Interferes with normal functioning of …

…Unsuitable and unfit to/for …

…Made crude attempt to …

…Unsuitable to/for …

…Behavior has declined to the point of …

…Has a strong moral weakness in …

…Suffers frequent minor setbacks because of …

…Failure to pay attention to detail caused …

…Has made insignificant progress in …

…Lags behind contemporaries in …

…Unable to take full advantage of …

…A major cause of disappointment because …

…Unable to grasp …

…Acts in haste without due regard to/of …

…Lacks mental restraint to …

…Suffered the loss of …

…Open distrust of subordinates causes …

…Strongly opposed to …

…Lacks knowledge or comprehension to …

…Lacks necessary wisdom and judgment to …

…Does not possess sufficient knowledge of …

…Made false statements concerning …

…Failed to act with promptness in/when …

…Sometimes uses ethically dubious means to …

…Incompetent in area(s) of …

…Without inner discipline to …

…Lacks the emotional stability to …

…Lax in complying and enforcing …

…Displayed improper judgment by/when …

…Refused to accept assistance to …

…Does not possess the necessary self-confidence to …

…Shows a marked unwillingness to …

…Careless and negligent in …

…Shows only artificial interest in …

…Deliberate lack of consideration for …

…Does not have the ability to …

…Excitable temper frequent cause of …

…Not accomplished or skilled in/at …

…Complete absence of …

…Chronic personal problems led to …

…Despite ample opportunity, failed to …

…Critically undermines morale by …

…Impeded work and discipline by …

…Sometimes lax in …

…Does not totally comply with …

…Requires routine reminders to …

…Inconsistent and unimpressive performance led to …

…Attitude and performance not in tune with …

…Usually drops behind others in/when …

…Fails to grasp the essentials of …

…Has a bad habit of …

…Stirs up trouble by …

…Exaggerated ego problem results in …

…Helpless when confronted with …

…Has great difficulty in/with …

…Relinquishes control over subordinates if/when …

…Has chronic weakness of/in …

…Prone to substandard work because of …

…Inconsistent and irregular work habits caused by …

…Not mentally equipped to …

…Occasionally regresses to old habits of …

…Personal indecision sometimes hinders …

…Acts without due consideration to/for …

…Becomes easily distracted by …

…Cannot control urge to …

…Sometimes uses excessive force to …

…Actions and deeds in sharp contrast with …

…Barely satisfactory in ability to …

…Compounds existing problems by …

…Inattention to duty caused …

…Belabors on nonessential matters a detriment to …

…A constant threat to morale by …

…Finds it most difficult to …

…Inexperienced in matters of …

…Displays marked indifference in/as …

…Not serious about …

…Personal desires frequently at contrast with …

…Totally inexperienced in/as …

…Has a distorted view of …

…Apathetic towards …

…Unable to fall in line with …

…Relieved of duties for cause when …

…Suppresses subordinate growth potential by …

…Superiors lost trust in abilities when …

…Tries to do a good job, but is hindered by …

…Utterly helpless when it comes to …

…Has no idea how to …

…Creates a bad relationship with co-workers because …

…Lacks vigor and persistence required to …

…Management plans are marred by …

…Not reliable to work independently because of …

…Loses control of/when …

…Becomes easily detached from job by …

…Inability to act decisively caused …

…Has difficulty dealing with others because …

…Misguided efforts caused …

…Produced minimal improvement despite …

…Exercised bad judgment in/by …

…Strays from strict compliance of rules if/when …

…Does not support …

…Experienced isolated incidences of …

…Of little value when/if …

...Decimated morale by/when ...

...No potential for future ...

...Failed to achieve consistency in ...

...Relieved of duties because ...

...Time after time proved a burden to ...

...Positive aspects of performance out weighed by ...

...Suffered loss of confidence in/by ...

...Unable to deal with reality of ...

...Unable to successfully ...

...Spends an inordinate amount of time in/on ...

...Lacks requisite knowledge in/to ...

...Has a noticeable imperfection in ...

...A lack of interest and concern for ...

...Has a predisposition toward ...

...Unable to deal with ...

...Has difficulty with ...

...Struggles to maintain correct balance of ...

...Despite noble intentions, unable to ...

...Planned badly for ...

...Frequently in discord with ...

…Failed to make satisfactory headway in …

…Has not kept pace with …

…Has emotional difficulty in coping with …

…Exercised bad judgment in/by …

…Not in compliance with …

.

PERFORMANCE

DICITONARY

PERFORMANCE

DICITONARY

This section contains 2000 of the most frequently used words in the English language to explain, state, define, or demonstrate individual performance or character. A brief definition/meaning is also provided.

For expanded use, a drafter can use the definition of the words.

WORD	CLASS	DEFINITION

A = Adjective   N = Noun   V = Verb

-A-

WORD	CLASS	DEFINITION
Abase	V	Loss of esteem
Aberrant	A/N	Substandard behavior
Abet	V	Encourage
Abhorrent	A	Disagreeable
Abide	V	Tolerate or accept
Ability	N	Skill, competence
Able	A	Capable, have ability
Abnormal	A	Not normal
Abrasive	A	Irritating
Abreast	A	At standard, even
Abrupt	A	Cut short without warning
Absentminded	A	Drifting of the mind
Absolute	A	Without doubt, fault
Abstract Thought	N	Theoretical thought process
Absurd	A	Obviously, clearly ridiculous
Abundant	A	Plenty
Abuse	N	Be improper, misuse
Abuse	V	Improper, misuse
Acceptable	A	Allowable, passable
Acclaim	V	Praise. Hold in high esteem
Acclaim	N	To praise
Accolade	N	Praise or acclaim
Accommodate	V	Allow. Make room. Fit
Accommodating	A	Beneficial, help

Accomplished	A	Skilled
Accost	V	Confront aggressively
Accurate	A	Correct
Ace	A	Top quality
Achieve	V	Accomplish, reach
Achievement	N	Something achieved
Achiever	N	One who achieves
Acme	N	The top, highest point
Activation	N	Make or cause action
Acuity	N	Keen, acute
Acumen	N	Perceptive, quickness
Acute	A	Keen or sharp
Acuteness	N	Agile, keen mind
Adamant	A	Not moving or flexible
Adept	A/N	Expert, skilled
Adequate	A	Satisfactory
Adhere	V	Stick to. Abide by
Adherence	N	Stick to. Abide by
Admirable	A	In high esteem, acclaim
Admire	V	Hold in high esteem
Adolescent	A	Not mature. Immature
Adroit	A	Skillful
Adverse	A	Opposed or opposing
Adversity	N	Bad situation
.Advocate	V	To support or back
Affable	A	Gets along with others

Agree	V	In accord. Agreement
Agreeable	A	Likable, pleasant
Aggressive	A	Forceful, intense
Agile	A	Skillful and flexible
Agile-minded	A	Mental dexterity, quickness
Agility	N	Being quick and agile
Agitate	V	Incite or fuel
Agitator	N	Someone who incites
Agog	A	Excitement, anticipation
Alacrity	N	Ready and willing
Alert	A	Perceptive
All-around	A	Versatile, multi-faceted
Altercation	N	Heated, aggressive argument
Ambiguity	N	Not definite or precise
Ambiguous	A	Not definite or precise. Obscure
Ambivalent	A	Indecisive, not firm
Amenity	N	Friendly
Amiable	A	Likable
Amicable	A	Likable, harmonious
Amity	N	Harmonious
Amiss	A	Awry, wrong
Analyze	V	Study part by part, in detail
Analytic	A	Skillful, discernible
Analytical	A	Logical analysis
Animate	V	Show zest and action
Animator	N	Active person. Puts into Action
Antagonist	N	One who agitates another
Antagonistic	A	Agitating

Antagonize	V	To agitate, incite
Anticipate	V	Expect
Antisocial	A	Not social
Anxious	A	Eager
Anxiousness	N	Anxious, apprehensive. Eager
A1	A	The best. Number one
Apathetic	A	Without interest
Apathy	N	Being without interest
Apex	N	The uppermost or highest point
Aplomb	N	Under control
Appall	V	Dismay. Disagreeable
Appalling	A	Be in dismay. Disagreeable
Appealing	A	Pleasing
Appease	V	To quell or quiet
Applaud	V	Show agreement, approval
Apt	A	Quick to grasp, learn
Aptitude	N	Ability, gift
Aptness	N	Quick to grasp, learn
Ardent	A	Strong, passionate
Arduous	A	Hard, strenuous, difficult
Arouse	V	Excite to action
Arrogance	N	Overbearing
Arrogant	A	Overbearing. Feeling egotistical
Artful	A	Of much skill, ability
Articulate	A	Clear, effective. Highly skilled
Artistic	A	Skillful thought, action

Artistic Imagination	N	Skillful, artful mental vision
Arousal	N	Move, spark to action
Askew	A	Not normal. Awry. Slanted
Aspiration	N	High ambition
Aspire	V	Attempt to reach
Assert	V	To compel or compelling
Assertive	A	Compel, compelling
Asset	N	Something owned of value
Astray	A	Move from correct, right
Astute	A	Mental alertness
Attitude	N	Mental disposition
Attribute	N	Possessed trait, ability
Audacious	A	Bold, venturesome
Audacity	N	Overly bold
Auspicious	A	Favorable, successful
Autocratic	A	Self rule. Not democratic
Aversion	N	Avoid
Avid	A	Extreme and intense
Avoid	V	Keep away from
Avow	V	Acknowledge
Aware	A	To have knowledge, know
Awareness	N	Be aware. Have knowledge
Awe	N	Mixed feelings
Awry	A	Wrong. Not right, correct

Baffle	V	Confuse, Mix up
Balk	V	Hesitate, delay
Banner	A	Above others
Bashful	A	Introvert, shy
Behavior	N	Conduct, manner
Belittle	V	Make little, small
Belligerence	N	Being aggressive. Hostile
Belligerent	A	Aggressive, hostile
Beneficial	A	Of use, benefit
Benevolence	N	Kind disposition
Benevolent	A	Kind or charitable
Benign	A	Good-natured
Berate	V	Scold violently
Berserk	N/A	Violent, reckless action
Betray	V	To violate, Go against
Bias	V	Predetermined. Bent. Swayed
Big-hearted	A	Giving, caring
Bland	A	Dull, uninteresting
Blemish	N	To mar or scar
Blithe	A	Gay, cheerful
Blunder	V	To mistake, error
Blunt	A	Abrupt. Over candid
Boisterous	A	Openly noisy or rowdy
Bold	A	Forward. Without reservation
Bold imagination	N	Daring, confident mental powers
Bolster	V	Support. Enforce. Back

Brainchild	N	Product of one's mental thought
Brainstorm	N	Fresh, new sudden ideas
Brain Trust	N	Subject experts
Brash	A	Bold and harsh
Brassy	A	Bold impudence, Brash
Brevity	N	Brief, to the point
Bright	A	Quick, keen mind
Brilliance	N	Bright, keen intellect
Brilliant	A	Great. Bright
Brisk	A	Lively. Energetic

-C-

Calculating	A	Shrewd, cunning
Callous	A	Insensitive
Camaraderie	N	Loyal friendship
Candid	A	Frank. Open
Capable	A	Possessing the ability
Capitalize	V	Use to advantage
Carefree	A	Without care
Careful	A	Attention to detail
Careless	A	Without attention to detail
Catalyst	N	Spark, stimulus for great change
Categorical	A	Without boundaries
Categorize	V	To classify
Ceiling	N	Top. Upper most
Censure	V	Condemn, criticize
Certain	A	Correct or true
Certainty	N	True without doubt

201

Chagrin	N	Disappointment in mind
Challenging	A	Prompting or stirring action
Champion	V	Lead or uphold
Chaos	N	Unorganized activity
Charade	N	Deceit. Hidden
Charisma	N	Magnetic leadership
Charismatic	A	Magnetic leadership
Charm	V	Appealing, personable
Charmer	N	Someone with charm, appeal
Charming	A	Greatly appealing or personable
Chastise	V	Censure or punish
Cheerful	A	Happy, gay
Circumvent	V	Go around
Clairvoyance	N	Extraordinary perceptive powers
Clairvoyant	A	Extraordinarily perceptive
Clarity	N	Clear, lucid
Clear-cut	A	Clear. Not ambiguous
Clear-headed	A	Clear knowledge
Clear-sighted	A	Clear, understanding thought
Clear-witted	A	Clear, keen mental faculty
Clever	A	Skillful wit
Cleverness	N	Quick, clever wit
Cocksure	A	Overconfidently sure
Cocky	A	Too self-confident
Coerce	V	Compel through strength
Cogent	A	Convince through strength

Cogitate	V	Deep meditation, thought
Cognition	N	Of deep thought
Cognizance	N	Knowledge. Information
Cohere	V	Hold together
Coherence	N	Consistency of mind, thought
Coherent	A	Holding or remaining together
Cohesion	N	Hold together firmly
Cohesive	A	Held together firmly
Cohort	N	Associate. Companion
Cold	A	Lacking in humanity
Collapse	V	Fall or fail
Colorless	A	Lacking in personality
Colossal	A	Exceptionally large
Comfort	N	Caring aid
Commend	V	To merit commendation
Commendation	N	Complimentary merit
Commitment	N	Obligation
Commonplace	N	Ordinary or routine
Common sense	N	Judgment with or without logic
Compassion	N	Humane sympathy
Compassionate	A	Humane sympathy
Compatible	A	Agreeable. Be, fit together
Compel	V	To make unavoidable
Compelling	A	Demanding
Competent	A/N	Capable, able
Competitive	A	Challenging. Competition
Competitor	N	One who challenges
Complacency	N	Satisfied to a fault

Complacent	A	Satisfied to a fault
Complaisant	A	Overly obliging
Complexity	N	Difficult. Complex
Complex	A	Hard to integrate or answer
Compliance	N	Comply. In accord
Complicate	V	Add difficulty
Complicated	A	Difficult, complex
Compliment	N	Give recognition
Comply	V	Adhere or conform
Comportment	N	Personal bearing
Composed	A	Calm, under control
Composure	N	Calmness
Comprehend	V	Understand
Comprehension	A	Understandable
Comprehension	N	To grasp, understand, know
Comprehensive	A	Extensive or inclusive
Compulsive	A	uncontrollable urge
Conceal	V	Cover, hide or omit
Concede	V	Give in. Accept. Agree
Conceivable	A	Imaginable in thought
Conceive	V	To think up
Concentrate	V	Direct, control thought process
Concentrating	A	Focusing one's mental powers
Conception	N	Mentally conceiving
Conceptive	A	Ability to mentally conceive
Conceptual	A	Mental grasp, conception

Conceptualize	V	Mentally conceive, formulate
Concern	N	Of interest
Concise	A	Brief and exact
Condemn	V	Find at fault
Condescend	V	To degrade, descend lower
Condescendence	N	Act of degrading. Patronize
Condescending	A	Degrading
Confidence	N	Assured belief
Conflict	N	At opposition
Conflicting	A	In opposition
Conform	V	In compliance, agreement
Conformance	N	Acceptable compliance
Conformity	N	Be in compliance
Confront	V	Openly challenge
Confuse	V	Not in order
Confusion	N	Mixed up
Confute	V	Refute. False. Useless
Congenial	A	Genial. Friendly
Congruent	A	Agreement. Harmony
Congruity	N	In agreement. Harmony
Congruous	A	Harmonious agreement
Conjecture	N	Assumption. Something assumed
Conscious	A	Knowing self-awareness
Consciousness	N	Self-awareness
Consistent	A	Steady and regular
Consonance	N	Harmonious. Agreement
Consonant	A	Harmony. In accord
Conspire	V	Plot, plan, act together

Constructive Imagination	N	Positive mental creativity
Consummate	A	Complete. Perfect
Contagious	A	Infectious. Spread to others
Contemplate	V	Deep thought. Ponder
Contempt	N	Having ill-feelings
Contemptible	A	Ill-feelings
Contribute	V	Give. Provide. Assist
Contribution	N	To give, provide
Contrive	V	Formulate with deep thought
Controversy	N	Debate. Dispute
Conventional	A	Standard. Routine
Conversant	A	Knowledgeable
Converse	V	Talk. Communicate
Convey	V	Get meaning across
Convincing	A	To win agreement
Cope	V	Able to handle, deal with
Cordial	A	Friendly and sociable
Correct	A	Without error
Corrupt	A	Not pure. Improper
Corruption	N	Not pure. Improper conduct, action
Courage	N	Strength or will to overcome
Courageous	A	Displaying courage, bravery
Courteous	A	Consideration
Courtesy	N	Considerate behavior
Cover-up	N	Hide. Not disclose
Craftiness	N	Sly, devious cunning

Crafty	A	Sly. Cunning
Crass	A	Without intelligent decency
Create	V	Conceive. Originate
Creative	A	Create. Originate. Invent
Creative Ability	N	Intellectual creative power
Creative Imagination	N	Intellectual creativeness
Creativeness	N	Creative intellect
Creative Power	N	Ability to originate, create
Creative Thought	N	Mental ability to create
Creativity	N	Able to create, originate, invent
Credential	N	Reputation or supportive fact
Credibility	N	Believable
Credible	A	Believed
Crimp	V	Hinder, impede, slow down
Crisis	N	Extremely important
Crisp	A	Terse. Clear
Critical	A	Extremely important
Criticize	V	Announce faults
Crucial	A	Critical. Important
Crude	A	Rough. Crass. Unrefined
Crusty	A	Ill-mannered. Rough
Cultivate	V	Nurture. Ignite. Spur on
Cultivated	A	Well refined, developed
Cultured	A	Refined, polished manner
Cumbersome	A	Hard to manage or wield
Cunning	A	Sharp, Sly skill
Curiosity	N	Interest. Inquisitive
Curious	A	Keenly interested. Inquisitive

Cursory	A	Brief view or interest
Curt	A	Abrupt and offensive
Customary	A	Routinely. Commonly. Usually
Cynical	A	Unbelieving with bad attitude

-D-

Dabble	V	Superficial involvement
Daunt	V	Unnerve. Discourage. Dismay
Dauntless	A	Unnerving. Intimidating
Debase	V	To lessen or diminish
Deception	N	Mislead. Trick
Deceptive	A	Mislead. Trick
Decisive	A	Without doubt or question
Decorum	N	Respectable behavior or dress
Deduction	N	Evaluate with logic
Deductive Power	A	Evaluate by logical reasoning
Deductive Power	N	Ability to logically reason
Deep-Thinking	A	Deep, profound intellect
Defect	N	Error. Fault
Defective	A	Having error or fault
Defiance	N	Go against. Oppose
Defiant	A	Against. Oppose
Deficient	A	Shortcoming. Missing something
Degradation	N	Belittle. Lower. Degrade
Degrade	V	Lower. Belittle. Take away
Deliberation	A	Full, due consideration

Delude	V	Mislead. Trick. Deceive
Delve	V	Dig into. Research
Demean	V	Belittle. Lessen. Lower
Demeanor	N	Behavior
Demerit	N	Without merit, good
Demise	N	Loss. Decline. Failure
Demoralize	V	Great drop in morale
Demure	A	Shy. Modest
Denounce	V	Publicly criticize
Dense	A	Slow to pick up, comprehend
Depend	V	Rely on
Dependable	A	Reliable. Trustworthy
Dependence	N	Dependent or relied upon
Dependency	N	Something needing assistance
Dependent	A	Depend or rely on
Depress	V	Disheartened. Discourage
Depressed	A	Disheartened. Sad
Deprive	V	Do without
Derelict	A	Improper attention
Dereliction	N	Knowing improper attention
Despair	V	Lose hope. Give up
Despairing	A	Without hope. Despair
Desperate	A	Without hope. Despair
Despond	V	Become without hope
Despondency	N	Being without hope
Despondent	A	Great hopelessness
Destroy	V	Ruin. Tear down
Deter	V	To thwart or turn

Deteriorate	V	Become less, lower
Determination	N	Firm resolve, conviction
Determined	A	Firmly committed
Detriment	N	Ill-being. To damage
Detrimental	A	Damaging. Ill-being
Deviant	A	Change downward or for worse
Deviate	A/N/V	Changing from the normal
Devious	A	Conniving, sly deviation
Devise	V	Originate. Invent
Devoted	A	Loyal. Faithful
Dexterity	N	Mental or physical agility
Dexterous	A	Mental or physical agility
Diction	N	Verbally clear, correct
Diehard	N	Decidedly against something
Die-hard	A	Positively against something
Differentiate	V	Distinguish difference
Difficult	A	Hard. Demanding
Difficulty	N	Being hard, demanding
Diffident	A	Self-confident
Dignity	N	High esteem. Praiseworthy
Dilute	V	Lessen. Reduce
Diminish	V	To lessen or reduce
Diplomacy	N	Skillfully tactful
Diplomat	N	Someone skillfully tactful
Diplomatic	A	Using tact with skill
Dire	A	Desperate. Distressful

Disaccord	V	Not in accord or agreement
Disadvantage	N	Not to advantage
Disagree	V	Against. Opposed
Disagreeable	A	Being against or opposed
Disagreement	N	At opposition. Against
Disappoint	V	Not to expectation, as expected
Disappointing	A	Not as expected
Disappointment	N	To disappoint, not succeed
Disaster	N	Great disorder
Discern	V	Skillful understanding or judgment
Discernible	A	Mentally recognize and separate
Discerning	A	Skillful understanding or judgment
Discipline	N	Self-control. Enforced control
Discontent	N	Not content or pleased
Discord	N/V	Failure to get along
Discourse	A	Verbally communicating
Discourteous	A	Not courteous, kind
Discredit	N	Without credit, belief
Discreet	A	Prudent judgment
Discriminating	A	Recognize. Distinguish difference
Disdain	N/V	Low in regard. At distance
Disdainful	A	Showing low regard
Disfavor	N	Not in favor, good standing
Disgruntle	V	Not happy, satisfied
Disgust	V	Sharp disapproval. Dislike
Disgust	N	At sharp disapproval, dislike
Disillusion	N	Not content, satisfied
Disinclined	A	Not approving or agreeing

211

Disloyal	A	Not loyal, trustworthy
Disloyalty	N	Without loyalty
Dismay	N/V	Disheartened. Disappoint
Disorder	N	Not in order
Disparity	N	A difference, fault
Dispassionate	A	Without passion, personal feeling
Dispute	V	Disagreement
Disregard	V	Without regard or attention
Disreputable	A	Bad reputation
Disrepute	N	Low reputation
Disrespect	N/V	Without respect
Disrupt	V	Break up or apart
Disruptive	A	Be out of order, routine
Dissatisfaction	N	Not satisfied, pleased
Dissatisfied	A	Not satisfied
Dissatisfy	V	Not satisfying
Dissension	N	Not in agreement
Dissent	N/V	Not in agreement
Dissenter	N	Someone who disagrees
Distinguished	A	With distinction. High esteem
Distort	V	Make cloudy, unclear, uncertain
Diverse	A	Varied. Multi-faceted
Docile	A	Passive. Highly receptive
Dodge	V	To go around. Evade
Dominant	A	Commanding or controlling
Dominate	V	To command, control over

Domineering	A	Prevail over, above
Drabber	A	Dull. Not lively
Dramatic	A	Extreme effect
Drastic	A	Major effect. Extreme. Harsh
Drive	N	Spur to action. Push. Urge
Drudge	V	Routine, recurring dull work
Drudging	A	Being routine and dull
Dubious	A	Questionable. Doubtful
Dull	A	Not mentally quick, perceptive
Dullness	N	Not mentally quick, perceptive
Durable	A	Long lasting without change
Duress	N	Under great pressure or strain
Dwindle	V	Continued decline
Dynamic	A	Powerful. Forceful

-E-

Eager	A	Ready. Zealous
Eager Beaver	N	Ready volunteer
Eagerness	N	Being ready, enthusiastic
Earnest	N	Sincere. Serious
Easygoing	A	Carefree. Little effort
Ebb	N/V	To recede. Diminish
Eccentric	A	Vary from norm, standard
Edit	V	Go over. Review
Editorialize	V	Communicate own opinion
Educable	A	Able to learn
Educate	V	Teach
Educated	A	Advanced education

213

Educator	N	A teacher
Effective	A	Obtain results. Satisfactory
Effervesce	V	Lively. Zestful
Effervescent	A	Liveliness. Zest. Zeal
Effete	A	Old. Obsolete
Efficiency	N	Doing without needless waste
Efficient	A	Without needless loss, waste
Effort	N	Attempt. Try
Effortless	A	Without effort, attempt
Ego	N	Self-esteem
Egocentric	A	Concerned with one's self
Egoism	N	Overly interested in one's self
Egoist	N	An ego person
Egotism	N	Overly self-centered
Elaborate	A	Go over in great detail
Elated	A	Elevated, high in thought
Elegance	N	Cultured. Respectable
Elegant	A	Greatly cultured, respectful
Elemental	A	Basic. Fundamental
Elementary	A	Basic elements
Elevated	A	Raised. Lifted
Elicit	V	Bring forward or out
Eloquence	N	Persuasive, fluent communications
Elucidate	V	Make clear, lucid
Elude	V	Avoid. Escape
Elusive	A	Avoid attention. Escape

Embitter	V	Bitter. Harsh
Embodiment	N	To encompass, embody something
Emerge	V	Come to view, focus
Embody	V	Encompass, incorporate, include
Eminent	A	Be, stand above
Emotion	N	Mental condition or state
Emotional	A	Expressed emotion
Empathetic	A	Humanely sensitive
Empathic	A	Exhibiting empathy
Empathize	V	Being humanely sensitive
Empathy	N	Humanely sensitive
Emphasize	V	Point out with strong attention
Emphatic	A	Express actively and zealously
Employ	V	Use. Occupy
Emulate	V	Imitate. Try to copy
Emulation	N	To imitate, copy, duplicate
Enable	V	Make able, ready
Enchant	V	Charm. Entice
Enchantment	N	Charmed. Enticing
Encourage	V	Prompt. Spur on
Encouragement	N	Prompting. Spurring
Encouraging	A	To encourage or prompt
Encumber	V	Burden. Weigh down
Encumbrance	N	Being burdened
Endeavor	N/V	Try. Attempt
Endless	A	Without end. Unending
Endurable	A	Able to last
Endurance	N	To last or hold up

Endure	V	to last, hold up
Energetic	A	Zeal. Vim. Vigor
Energize	V	Make energetic
Energy	N	Having zeal, vim, vigor
Enervate	A/V	Without vim, vigor
Enforce	V	Give force. To back
Engaging	A	Attracting. Pleasant
Engender	V	Initiate. Foster. Spur
Engrossing	A	Engaging. Involving
Enhance	V	Help. Promote. Add to
Enigma	N	Confusing. Hard to understand
Enjoy	V	Like. Please
Enjoyment	N	Being at joy. Pleasing
Enlighten	V	Bring to light. Inform
Enlightened	A	Brought to light. Informed
Enlightenment	N	To enlighten
Enmity	N	Deep, bad feeling or will
Enormous	A	Great amount, size
Enrage	V	Angry. Furious
Enrich	V	Add, contribute, or give to
Enterprise	N	Task or tasking. Project
Enterprising	A	Energetic, vigorous, and ready
Entertain Ideas	V	Open to suggestion, thought
Enthuse	V	Inspire. Excite
Enthusiasm	N	Inspiring. Exciting
Enthusiast	N	Someone with enthusiasm

Enthusiastic	A	Being enthused
Entice	V	Skillfully tempt or excite
Entrust	V	To trust
Enunciate	V	Verbal dexterity, clarity
Enviable	A	Having worthy qualities
Envious	A	Possessing worthy qualities
Envision	V	See, think within
Epitome	N	Best. Ideal example
Epitomize	V	Idealize. Representative
Equable	A	Even. Consistent
Equality	N	Equal. On par. Even
Equitable	A	Being even, consistent
Equivocal	A	Not definite, certain
Equivocate	V	False. Vague
Eradicate	V	End. Finish off
Erode	V	Wear away. Tear down
Erosive	A	Able to erode
Errant	A	Stray. Wander
Erratic	A	Not regular, consistent
Erroneous	A	Error. Mistake
Error	N	Wrong. Incorrect Not true
Erudite	A	Learned. Skilled
Erudition	N	Highly learned, skilled
Erupt	V	Burst out, forward
Escalate	V	Heighten. Increase
Eschew	V	Shun. Go around
Esprit de corps	N	Strong common spirit, bond
Essential	A	Mandatory part or ingredient

Establish	V	Bring into being
Esteem	N	High regard. Honored
Ethic	N	Moral concepts or views
Ethical	A	In accord. Conformance
Etiquette	N	Social conduct
Euphoria	N	High in feeling
Evasive	A	Evading. Elusive
Exacerbate	V	Increase in harshness, bitterness
Exact	A	Precise. Without error
Exacting	A	Demanding. Correctness
Exaggerate	V	False or artificial largeness
Exalt	V	Favorable rise or raise
Exanimate	A	Without spirit
Exceed	V	Go beyond. Surpass
Exceeding	A	Going beyond. Surpassing
Excel	V	Surpass. Succeed
Excellence	N	High quality
Excellent	A	First rate. Top quality
Exceptional	A	Very top quality
Excessive	A	More than needed, required
Excitable	A	Capable of arousing
Excite	V	Arouse. Move to action
Excitement	N	Aroused. Moved to action
Exciter	N	One who excites
Exciting	A	Arousing. Stimulating
Exclusive	A	Strictly limited

Excuse	N	Reason. Explanation
Exemplary	A	Excellent. Finest quality
Exemplify	V	Embody. An example
Exhort	V	Incite. Urge
Exonerate	V	Clear. Free
Exorbitance	N	Being exorbitant. In excess
Exorbitant	A	Too much. Excess
Expand	V	Increase. Grow
Expectation	N	Anticipate. Look forward
Expedience	N	Speed-up
Expediency	N	Speed up. Expedient
Expedient	A	Easiest choice
Expedite	V	Proceed immediately
Expeditious	A	To expedite, cause action
Experience	N	Learned earlier
Experienced	A	Knowledgeable. Skillful
Expert	A	Most experienced, skilled
Expertise	N	Possessing experience or skill
Explicit	A	Not ambiguous. Exact
Exploit	V	Make use of
Explore	V	Check into. Investigate
Explosive	A	Capable of erupting
Expostulate	V	Consider. Evaluate
Expound	V	Explain. Clarify. Put forth
Extensive	A	To great extent
Extenuate	V	Reduce. Lessen
Extra	A	More. Additional
Extraneous	A	Extra. More than enough

Extraordinary	A	Extra to, or above ordinary
Extravagant	A	More than necessary, required
Extreme	A	Beyond reasonable
Exuberance	N	Being exuberant, enthused
Exuberant	A	Enthused. Lively. Zealous
Exultant	A	Extreme joy, high thrill
Eyesore	N	Repulsive to see

-F-

Fabricate	V	Make. Make up
Fabulous	A	Great almost beyond belief
Facetious	A	Unsuccessful wit
Facile	A	Superficial. Without substance
Facilitate	V	Aid. Assist
Facility	N	Aptitude. Ability. Skill
Factual	A	Truthful. Actual
Faculties	N	Possessed ability or capacity
Faculty	N	Possessed skill, ability
Fade	V	Decrease, lessen with time
Fail	V	Without success or gain
Failure	N	Perform without success
Fair	A	Without bias or prejudice
Fair play	N	Equal and fair
Fair-spoken	A	Light or soft spoken
Faith	N	Belief. Believe in
Faithful	A	True in faith
Faithless	A	Without truth or faith

220

Fake	N/V	Imposter. Not true
False	A	Not true or correct
Falsify	V	Make untrue or incorrect
Falsity	N	At or being false
Falter	V	Hesitate. Fall short
Fantastic	A	Great. Almost beyond belief
Farcical	A	Ridiculous. Laughable
Farfetched	A	Far out. Hard to believe
Far-reaching	A	Wide or long reaching
Farseeing	A	See far ahead
Farsighted	A	See or plan far ahead
Fascinating	A	Enchanting. Engaging
Fascination	N	Being enchanted
Fastidious	A	Overly demanding
Fatigue	N	Worn down or out
Fatuity	N	Extremely simple
Fatuous	A	Simple. Inane
Fault	N	Error. Wrong. Fail
Faultfinding	A/N	Predetermined to find fault
Faultless	A	Without fault or wrong
Faulty	A	Having fault, error
Favorable	A	Agreeable. Approving
Favoritism	N	Showing bias or favor
Fearful	A	In fear from danger
Fearless	A	Without fear. Bold
Feasible	A	Allowable. Acceptable

Feat	N	Good, great deed or act
Feckless	A	Without responsibility
Fecund	A	Fertile & productive intelligence
Feeble	A	Weak. Frail
Feebleminded	A	Mentally lacking, deficient
Feeling	A	Emotion. Belief
Feisty	A	Anxious. Exuberant
Felicitous	A	Talk with poise. Suitable
Felicity	N	Cheerful. Happy
Fellowship	N	Camaraderie. Friendship
Fend	V	Defend. Do without assistance
Fertile	A	Reservoir of ability, thought
Fertile Mind	N	Highly productive mind
Fervent	A	Feeling of friendly warmth
Fervor	N	Great passion, emotion
Festive	A	Joyous. Happy. Active
Fetter	N	Restrain
Feud	N	Long-standing dislike, disagreement
Feverish	A	At a hot pace
Fiasco	N	Utter failure
Fickle	A	Not consistent, constant, resolute
Fiction	N	Not true or real
Fictitious	A	Being untrue or unreal
Fidelity	N	Faithful. In accord
Fiduciary	A	State of high trust
Fierce	A	Intense, active hostility
Fiery	A	Hot, active emotion
Figurehead	N	Not actual. In name only

Finagle	V	Deceit. False. Trick
Fine	A	Good. Excellent
Finely	A	Extremely fine
Finesse	N	Mental skill, agility and ability
Fine-tune	V	Fine adjustment for best operation
Finicky	A	Too exacting or petty
Finite	A	Limited. Not infinite
Firm	A	Resolute. Unmoving
First	N	Top. Highest. Best
First Class	N	Classed top, highest, first
First-rate	A	First or top quality
First-string	A	First rate
Five-star	A	Best. Tops
Fizzle	N	Fade. Fail
Flagged	A	Weak. Without zeal
Flagrant	A	Openly blatant, disagreeable
Flair	N	Special knack or skill. Ability
Flappable	A	Not sure, confident
Flashy	A	Superficial. Words without deeds
Flaunt	V	Open defiance. Bold
Flaw	N	Not correct, perfect
Fledgling	N	New. Not mature
Flexibility	N	Adaptable. Not rigid
Flexible	A	Adaptable. Able to alter, change
Flimsy	A	Not firm, solid. Weak
Flip-flop	N	Not firm. Changes views, opinions

Flop	V	Fail
Flounder	V	Hesitate. Lose way, direction
Flourish	V	Thrive. Excel
Flout	V	Open defiance
Fluctuate	V	Move back & forth. Oscillate
Fluent	A	Skilled. Learned
Fluid	A	Smooth flowing
Flunk	V	Fail. Flop
Fluster	N	Thwart. Discourage
Flutter	N	Uncertain, non-directed motion
Focus	N	Center-in. Key in on
Foible	N	Fault. Error
Foil	V	Stop. Prevent
Follower	N	One who follows. Not a leader
Folly	N	Foolish
Foolhardy	A	Ill-advised
Foolish	A	Lack of proper judgment
Foolishness	N	Act of improper judgment
Foolproof	A	Without chance of error, fault
Foot-dragging	N	Deliberate slowness
Foppish	A	Overly self-concerned, vain
Forbidding	A	Refraining. Prohibiting
Force	N	Driving power, influence, strength
Forceful	A	Using force. Exerting pressure
Forcible	A	Able to be forceful
Foremost	A	At the front, top
Foresee	V	See forward, ahead
Foresight	N	See ahead. Plan ahead

Foresighted	A	Mentally see ahead, future
Foresightedness	N	Mentally see ahead, future
Forestall	V	To stop or obstruct
Forfeit	N/V	Give up or away
Forget	V	Fail to remember
Forgetful	A	Failing to remember
Forgive	V	to let pass. Excuse
Forgiveness	N	Letting pass. Excusing
Forgiving	A	To forgive, overlook
Formality	N	Official procedure
Formalize	V	Make formal, official, complete
Formative	A	Developing. Growing
Formidable	A	Very difficult, discouraging
Formless	A	Without form, order, or shape
Formulate	V	Develop. Put together
Forte	N	Someone's best trait
Forthright	A	Direct. Frank. Open
Fortify	V	To strengthen, build up
Fortitude	N	Mental strength and persistence
Fortuitous	A	By accident, chance
Fortunate	A	Lucky. Favorable
Forum	N	Free discussion
Forward-looking	A	Look and plan ahead
Foul-up	N	Botch. Bungle
Foundation	N	Base or founding frame
Founder	V	Fail. Fall. Decline

Four-star	A	Top grade, quality
Fracas	N	Noisy confrontation
Factious	A	Unruly. Difficult to control
Fragile	A	Weak. Not strong. Frail
Fragment	N	A part, piece of something
Fragmentary	A	Not complete. In parts
Frail	A	Weak. Not strong
Frank	A	Open, forward manner
Frantic	A	Fast, unorganized pace
Fraud	N	Knowing deceit
Fraudulent	A	Being or doing deceit
Free-spoken	A	To openly candid. Speak freely
Freethinker	N	Unrestrained, independent thinking
Freewill	A	Spontaneous. Unrestrained
Frenzy	N	Unthinking, violent action
Frequent	A	Often. At great frequency
Fresh	A	New energy, vigor
Fret	V	Worry. Concerned
Friction	N	Disagree. Oppose
Friendly	A	Amicable. Kind disposition
Friendly	N	Someone friendly
Frivolous	A	Without importance or value
Fruitful	A	Productive. Successful
Fruitless	A	Non-productive. Without gain
Frustrate	V	Thwart. Ineffective
Frustrated	A	Being thwarted or ineffective
Frustration	N	Being frustrated
Fulfill	V	Accomplish. Complete

Full-fledged	A	Fully completed
Full-scale	A	Maximum limit or scale
Fumble	V	Blunder. Clumsy
Fundamental	A	Basic, central elements
Furious	A	Great, heated anger
Furor	N	Furious. Angry
Fury	N	Anger. Rage
Fussy	A	Finicky. Overly particular
Futile	A	Worthless. Ineffective
Futility	N	Being futile
Fuzzy	A	Unclear. Not defined. Blurred

-G-

Gab	V	Talk too much
Gall	N	Boldness. Fortitude
Gallant	A	Bold. Energetic. Daring
Galling	A	Annoying. Boldness
Gamesmanship	N	Improper advantage or tactics
Garrulity	N	Idle, insignificant talk
Garrulous	A	Too much idle, Insignificant talk
Gauche	A	Social non acceptance
Generalize	V	Vague. Broadly defined
Generate	V	Start. Instill
Generous	A	Kind. Giving. Caring
Genial	A	Kind, sympathetic personality

Genius	N	Innate superior intellect
Genteel	A	Polite. Poised. Polished
Gentle	A	Soft. Kind
Genuine	A	Actual. Real
Gesture	N	Express by body movement
Gift	N	Talent
Gifted	A	Great natural intellect
Gigantic	A	Extremely large, big
Gimmick	N	Shrewd device or scheme
Gingerly	A	Tenderly, tentative
Gist	N	Major thought or idea. Overview
Glad	A	Happy. Cheerful. Gay
Glaring	A	Glowing. Gross. Obvious
Glitch	N	Problem. Trouble. Setback
Gloom	V	Dark, bleak in outlook
Gloomy	A	Bleak, depressed outlook
Glorify	V	Make or add glory
Glorious	A	Having, or being, glory
Glory	N	High in honor, esteem
Glum	A	Bleak. Gloomy
Good	A./N	Favorable. Positive
Good deal	N	Great amount
Good faith	N	Earnest in faith
Good-for-nothing	A	Wirth nothing. Without value
Good-hearted	A	Kind at heart. Kind hearted
Good-humored	A	Positive, cheerful manner
Goodly	A	Great amount
Good-natured	A	Pleasant, helpful manner

Goodwill	N	Caring and friendly
Gracious	A	Poised and charming. Thoughtful
Gradual	A	Changing, shifting over time
Grandeur	N	Being grand or grandiose
Grandiose	A	Overly impressive. Showy.
Gratify	V	Pleasing. Satisfying
Gratifying	A	Being pleasing, satisfying
Grave	A	Serious with harmful consequences
Gravity	N	Significant in importance
Great	A	Large. Significant. Remarkable
Greathearted	A	Generous and caring
Gregarious	A	Sociable
Grievance	N	Gripe. Complaint
Grieve	V	Grief. Sorrow
Grievous	A	Grave, serious, painful
Grim	A	Dark. Dreary. Unpleasant
Grimace	N	Disapprove by facial gesture
Grind out	V	To do methodically, mundane
Gripe	V	Complain. Object
Grit	N	Strong resolute courage
Gross	A	Bad. Flagrant
Grouse	V	Fault-finding. Complain
Grudge	N	Get back or even
Grudging	A	With reluctance
Grueling	A	Extremely strenuous or punishing
Guide	N/V	Oversee, supervise. Point the way

Guile	N	Crafty, cagy
Guileless	A	Without guile
Guise	N	False cover, front
Gumption	N	Common sense. Courage
Gung ho	A	Unbound enthusiasm
Gusto	N	Zeal, vigor, vim

-H-

Habitual	A	Recurring as by habit
Half-baked	A	Improper planning, forethought
Half-cocked	A	Improper planning, forethought
Halfhearted	A	Without full support
Half-scholar	A	Not learned, knowing
Half-truth	N	Deliberate less than full truth
Halo effect	N	Over grading based on few traits
Hamper	V	Interfere. Impede. Obstruct
Hands-on	A	Do physically. First hand
Haphazard	A/N	Without plan. By chance
Hapless	A	Happen without luck
Happenstance	N	By chance. Haphazard
Happy-go-lucky	A	Not properly concerned, caring
Harass	V	Continued bothering, troubling
Hard-and-fast	A	Firm. Fixed. Unyielding
Hardhanded	A	Overly strict, firm
Hardheaded	A	Unrelenting. Firm. Stubborn
Hard-hearted	A	Without humane concern, sympathy

Hard-nosed	A	Unrelenting. Firm. Stubborn
Hard put	A	With great difficulty
Hard-set	A	Unrelenting. Firm
Hard-shell	A	Not giving or compromising
Hardship	N	Great difficulty. Suffering
Harm	N/V	Cause damage, danger, hurt
Harmless	A	Without harm, damage, danger
Harmonious	A	Be in harmony
Harmony	N	Get along. No friction
Harsh	A	Severe. Coarse. Rough
Hasten	V	Speed up. Quicken
Hasty	A	Hurried. Quick. Fast
Hatred	N	To hate. Extreme dislike
Headlong	A	Without delay, hesitation
Headway	N	Gain. Progress
Headwork	N	Mental work. Think. Ponder
Hearsay	N	Not sure, proven fact
Heartfelt	A	In sincere sympathy
Heartless	A	Without heart, compassion
Hearty	A/N	Full. Complete. Sincere
Heavy-handed	A	Stern. Harsh. Overly demanding
Heavyhearted	A	Deepest sympathy. Deep felt
Heckle	V	Antagonize. Annoy. Impede
Hectic	A	Frantic. Fast-paced
Heed	N	To pay attention. Note
Heedful	A	to heed, take notice
Heedless	A	Without attention or heed
Helpless	A	Without help, assistance

Helpful	A	To assist, help. Cooperate
Heritage	N	Handed down over time
Herky-jerky	A	Inconsistent. Fluctuating
Hero	N	Held in highest esteem, thought
Hidden	A	Not shown. Out of sight
Hierarchy	N	Those higher in command or control
Higher education	N	Advanced or college education
Higher learning	N	Advanced or college learning
High-flying	A	Exuberant. Excessive
High-minded	A	High ideals, principles
High-powered	A	Powerful. Mighty
High-pressure	A	Great pressure. Tense. Demanding
High-spirited	A	Enthusiastic, energetic spirit
High-strung	A	Temperamental. Over bearing
High-toned	A	Arrogant. Elevated principles
Hinder	V	Impede. Hamper. Harm
Hindrance	N	to hinder, harm, hurt
Hindsight	N	Apply after-the-fact knowledge
Hit-or-miss	A	Be by chance. At random
Hone	V	To fine tune
Honest	A	True. Truthful. No deceit
Honesty	N	Being honest
Honor	N	High moral standard
Honorable	A	Having, deserving honor
Hope	V	Strong, positive desire
Hopeful	A	Having hope

Hopeless	A	Without hope, chance, desire
Horrendous	A	Extremely bad, distasteful
Hospitable	A	Friendly. Caring
Hostile	A	Not hospitable. Very unfriendly
Hostility	N	Aggressive, hostile conduct
Huge	A	Great many. Sizable
Humane	A	Caring, concerned, compassion
Humanitarian	N	Someone humane in thought, action
Humble	A	Submissive. Subordinate one's self
Humdrum	A	Without vim, vigor. Dull
Humiliate	V	To belittle or shame another
Humiliating	A	Demeaning. To humiliate
Humility	N	Being humble
Humor	N	Pleasing character
Humorless	A	Without humor
Humorous	A	Having humor, wit, charm
Hurdle	V	Go over. Not impede
Hurried	A	Rushed. Hastened
Hurtful	A	Doing harm, hurt, damage
Hygiene	N	Personal health, sanitation
Hyper	A	Easily agitated, excited
Hypercritical	A	Over critical

-I-

Idea	N	A thought from the mind
Ideal	A	Perfect. Exact. Precise
Ideal	N	Envisioned or sought goal
Idealist	N	Placing ideals ahead of reality

Idealistic	A	Concerning ideals
Idealize	A	Be ideal, representative
Idle	A	Not busy. Not doing
Ignite	V	Fire up. Start. Motivate
Ignorance	N	Having lack of knowledge
Ignorant	A	Not knowledgeable
Ignore	V	Avoid
Ill-advised	A	Not properly advised
Illaudable	A	Not laudable or praised
Illegal	A	Not legal or lawful
Illegible	A	Not legible, readable
Ill-fated	A	Predetermined bad fate
Ill-gotten	A	Illegal or improperly gotten
Ill-humored	A	Without humor
Illicit	A	Illegal
Illiteracy	N	Not literate. Not read or write
Illiterate	A	Not knowing, educated
Ill-mannered	A	Bad manners. Crude
Ill-natured	A	Bad attitude or nature
Illogic	N	Being without logic
Illogical	A	Not logical, reasonable
Illustrate	V	To show or make clear
Illustrious	A	Commendable actions
Image	V	Visualize. See in mind
Imagine	V	Mental picture, image
Imaginable	A	Able to imagine or visualize

Imaginary	A	Not real or fact
Imagination	N/A	Imagine, visualize in the mind
Imaginative	A	Unreal. Untrue
Imbalance	N	Not proper balance
Imitate	V	Copy. Duplicate
Imitation	N	Not real, fact, true
Immaculate	A	Without flaw. Pure
Immature	A	Not mature or completely developed
Immeasurable	A	Beyond measure
Immediacy	N	Being immediate
Immense	A	Vast. Huge. Large
Immensity	N	Being immense
Immerge	V	Immerse. Throw into completely
Immerse	V	Become totally absorbed, Involved
Immobile	A	Not mobile or movable. Fixed
Immobilize	V	Make immobile or fixed
Immoderate	A	Not moderate. Excess. Excessive
Immoral	A	Not moral. Against moral values
Immovable	A	Not movable. Fixed
Impair	V	Restrict, restrain, hinder
Imparity	N	Inequity. Uneven
Impart	V	Pass along. Communicate
Impassioned	A	Great passion, feeling
Impatience	N	Not patient. Anxious
Impatient	A	Not patient. Anxious
Impeccable	A	Without flaw or fault. Unblemished
Impede	V	Interfere. Harm or slow
Impel	V	Push or force forward

235

Impenetrable	A	Unable to penetrate, enter
Imperfect	A	Not perfect. Flawed. Error
Imperfection	N	Being not perfect. Flawed
Impersonal	A	Not personal. Not open, friendly
Impersonalize	V	Make impersonal
Impertinence	N	Be impertinent
Impertinent	A	Not appropriate, relevant
Impervious	Adj	Unable to penetrate, enter
Impetuous	A	Impulsive. Action on emotion
Impetus	N	Motivating, or driving force
Impious	A	Improper respect
Implicit	A	Exact, without question
Impolite	A	Not polite, socially acceptable
Imponderable	A	Beyond question, evaluation
Importance	N	Being important
Important	A	Of considerable value
Impose	V	Force or bring pressure to
Imposing	A	Impressively striking
Impossible	A	No possible or capable
Impossibility	N	To be impossible. Not capable
Impotent	A	Not potent. Unable
Impracticable	A	Not practicable, feasible
Impractical	A	Not practical, prudent or sensible
Imprecise	A	Not precise, correct. Ambiguous
Impress	V	Influence. Leave mark. Impact
Impressive	A	Able to impress

236

Impression	N	To influence or impact opinion
Impressionable	A	Easily impressed or influenced
Improbable	A	Unlikely. Not probable
Impromptu	A	Without prior plan
Improper	A	Not proper or correct
Impropriety	N	Being or doing improper
Improve	V	To make better
Improvement	N	Making or doing better
Improvisation	N	To improvise
Improvise	V	To make do. Impromptu
Imprudence	N	Not prudent, wise
Imprudent	A	Not wise or judicious
Imprudence	N	Being impudent
Impudent	A	Contemptible. Bold. Not reserved
Impugn	V	Aggressive, forceful attack
Impulsive	A	Act without thought
Impute	V	Accuse. Charge
Inability	N	Not able, capable
Inaccuracy	N	Not accurate, correct
Inaccurate	A	Not accurate, correct
Inaction	N	No action. Motionless
Inactive	A	Not active. Without movement
Inadequacy	N	Not adequate, sufficient
Inadequate	A	Not adequate, sufficient
Inadvertence	N	By accident, chance. Not intended
Inadvertent	A	By accident, chance. Not intended
Inadvisable	A	Not advised or recommended
Inane	A	Without substance or direction

Inappropriate	A	Not appropriate, acceptable
Inapt	A	Not apt, suitable
Inaptitude	N	Lack of aptitude, ability
Inarticulate	A	Not clear, precise in expression
Inattention	N/A	Not giving proper attention
Inborn	A	Born with. Natural
Inbred	A	Being in one's nature
Incalculable	A	Not able to calculate, determine
Incapable	A	Not capable, able
Incapacitate	V	Make not capable, able
Incapacity	N	Without capability or ability
Incentive	N	Something providing motive
Incertitude	N	Not certain, sure
Incisive	A	Most decisive, direct
Incite	V	Stimulate, move, urge
Incitement	N	Cause, arouse, action, movement
Inclination	N	Personal character
Incline	V	Lean. Favor
Inclined	A	Leaning. Favoring
Incogitant	A	Without thought or consideration
Incoherent	A	Missing in coherence or presence
Incomparable	A	Not comparable
Incompatibility	N	Not able to get along, mix
Incompatible	A	Unable to get along, mix
Incompetence	N	Not having capability or capacity
Incompetent	A	Without capability or capacity

Incomplete	A	Not finished, complete
Incomprehensible	A	Not imaginable, believable
Incomprehension	N	Unable to understand, grasp
Inconceivable	A	Unable to convince, persuade
Inconclusive	A	Not conclusive, final, complete
Incongruous	A	Not in step, agreement
Inconsequent	A	Not planned, resulting from logic
Inconsequential	A	Of little importance, matter
Inconsiderable	A	Of little value or worth
Inconsiderate	A	Not considerate of others
Inconsistency	N	Being inconsistent
Inconsistent	A	Not constant, steady, same
Inconsonance	N	Not in agreement, accord
Inconspicuous	A	Not visible, noticeable
Incontestable	A	Without doubt or question
Incontrovertible	A	Not changeable, questionable
Inconvenience	N	Not convenient. Out of the way
Inconvenient	A	Out of the way
Incorrect	A	Not correct, true, right
Incorrigible	A	Not manageable. Not changeable
Incredible	A	Almost beyond belief
Incurable	A	Not changeable, curable
Indecision	N	Not decisive, resolute
Indecisive	A	Not decisive, final, complete
Indefectible	A	Without defect, fault, flaw
Indefensible	A	Unable to defend, justify, excuse
Indefinable	A	Unable to define, clarify
Indefinite	A	Not definite or precise

239

Independent	A	Along. Without assistance or aid
In-depth	A	Complete, comprehensive
Indestructible	A	Not able to destruct, destroy
Indifference	N	Being indifferent
Indifferent	A	Not concerned, caring
Indignant	A	Showing indignation
Indignation	N	Unjustified anger
Indignity	N	Without self-respect
Indirect	A	Not direct or straight
Indiscernible	A	Not identifiable, clear
Indiscipline	N	Without discipline, control
Indiscreet	A	Not discreet. Too open
Indiscretion	N	Not discreet, normal
Indiscriminate	A	Without logic, reason
Indispensable	A	Not able to do/be without
Indisputable	A	Without question. Absolutely
Indistinct	A	Not clear, distinct
Indistinctive	A	Not distinct
Individualist	N	One going or standing alone
Individuality	N	One's own character, self
Indoctrinate	V	Instruct, train in new areas
Indolent	A	Slow. Lazy
Induce	V	Indirect influence
Inducement	N	To induce, ignite
Indulge	V	Give in, submit
Indulgence	N	To indulge, submit

Indulgent	A	To indulge, submit
Indurate	V	Hard and fast. Unyielding
Industrious	A	Skillfully and productively active
Industry	N	Persistent pursuit
Ineffective	A	Not effective, or as expected
Ineffectual	A	Not effective, or as expected
Inefficacy	N	Without sufficient control, power
Inefficiency	N	Being inefficient
Inefficient	A	Not best use of resources
Ineligible	A	Not eligible, qualified
Ineloquent	A	Without eloquence
Inept	A	Not competent, fit
Ineptitude	N	Being inept
Inequality	N	Not equal, even
Inequitable	A	Not equitable, equal, even
Inequity	N	Not just, fair
Inerrant	A	Without error, fault, flaw
Inert	A	Not active. Slow
Inescapable	A	Unable to avoid, miss, omit
Inevitable	A	No chance of avoiding
Inexact	A	Not exact, correct. Error
Inexcusable	A	Unable to excuse, overlook
Inexhaustible	A	Unending. Without end
Inexorable	A	Unmoving. Relentless
Inexpedient	A	Not recommended, advisable
Inexperience	N	Without experience, training
Inexpert	A	Not expert, trained, skilled
Inexplicable	A	Without explanation, reason

Inexplicit	A	Not explicit, exact, correct
Inextinguishable	A	Unable to stop, end
Infallible	A	Not capable of mistake, error
Infect	V	Communicate to, get into
Infectious	A	To infect by spreading
Inferior	A	Below standard, par
Infinite	A	Without end. Unending
Inform	A	Weak. Not strong, sound
Inflame	V	To agitate, excite
Inflexible	A	Not movable, flexible. Rigid
Influence	N	Ability to control
Influential	A/N	To influence, control, power
Informal	A	Not formal, official
Informative	A	Communicate knowledge, info.
Informed	A	Knowing. Learned
Infraction	N	Violation of rule, law
Infrastructure	N	Basic foundation or framework
Infrequent	A	Not frequent. Rare
Infringe	V	Violate by entering, intruding
Infuriate	V	Make angry, mad
Infuse	V	Instill in someone, thing
Ingenious	A	Original in something genius
Ingenuity	N	Genius in originating, devising
Ingenuous	A	Open. Not complex, complicated
Ingrain	V	To instill, infuse. Put into
Ingrained	A	Deeply rooted within

Ingratitude	N	Not grateful in kind, return
Inharmonious	A	Not getting along, fitting in
Inharmony	N	Not in harmony, accord, agreement
Inhabit	V	Mental restraint, reluctance
Inhospitable	A	Not friendly
Inhumane	A	Not humane, caring
Inimical	A	Not friendly in nature, manner
Inimitable	A	Not able to duplicate
Inequity	N	Not just, fair. Biased
Initiate	V	To start, begin
Initiative	N	Acting without guidance, direction
Injudicious	A	Not judicious or appropriate
Injustice	N	Without justice, fairness
Innate	A	Possessed as natural, inner self
Innocent	A	Not wrong
Innovate	V	Originate new ways, means
Innovation	N	Doing something new, better
Innovative	A	To innovate
Innuendo	N	Subtle hint. Infer indirectly
Innumerable	A	Too many to number, count
Innumerous	A	Too many to number, count
Inopportune	A	Not opportune, convenient, timely
Inordinate	A	Beyond expected limit
Inquisitive	A	Seek information. Ask questions
Insatiable	A	Unending appetite. Never satisfied
Insensibility	N	Not perceptive, aware, knowing
Insensible	A	Not sensible, reasonable
Insensitive	A	Without feeling, caring

243

Insidious	A	Sly. Unsuspecting. Harmful
Insight	N	See into, through something
Insightful	A	Mental understanding
Insignificance	N	Not significant or meaningful
Insignificant	A	Not significant or meaningful
Insincere	A	Not sincere, honest, true
Insinuate	V	Subtle hint. Infer indirectly
Insipid	A	Dull and without interest
Insolence	N	Being overbearing, contemptible
Insolent	A	Overbearing. Being in contempt
Insolvable	A	Without solution, answer
Inspiration	N	Inspire others to do, act
Inspirational	A	Inspire. Influence
Inspire	V	Influence, prompt others to act
Inspired	A	Possess inspirational traits
Inspiring	A	Affecting in, to inspire
Inspirit	V	Have spirit
Instability	N	Not stable, sturdy, sound
Instantaneous	A	Without any delay
Instigate	V	To start, spur on, forward
Instill	V	To place in or put in
Instinctive	A	Already known, within. Built in
Instrumental	A	A key or important ingredient
Insubordinate	A	In violation of authority
Insubstantial	A	Not substantial, significant
Insufferable	A	Unable to tolerate

Insufficient	A	Not sufficient enough
Insult	V	Openly offend
Insult	N	Open indignity
Insuperable	A	Not able to overcome
Insupportable	A	Unable to support, defend
Insurgent	A	Opposed to authority
Insurmountable	A	Not able to overcome
Intangible	A	Not tangible, touchable
Integral	A	Essential, necessary part
Integrate	V	to bring together, combine
Integrative Power	N	Mental ability to sort, segregate
Integrity	N	In adherence. Abiding
Intellect	N	Mental capacity, ability
Intellection	N	Power, reason of thought
Intellectual	A/N	Mental power. Intellect
Intellectual Faculty	N	Mental, reasoning capability
Intellectual Grasp	N	Understand mentally
Intellectual Power	N	Mental ability
Intellectual Weakness	N	Mentally lacking, deficient
Intelligence	N	Mental ability, capacity
Intelligent	A	High mental ability, capacity
Intense	A	Extreme, extensive
Intercede	V	To come between
Interested	A	Curious, attentive, involved
Interfere	V	Hinder, harm by entering
Interference	N	Interfere, obstruct, hinder
Interfuse	V	Fuse together. Bind
Intermittent	A	Not regular, constant

Interpose	V	Place or put between
Interpret	V	Explain. Understand
Interrogate	V	Question at length
Interrupt	V	to break, cease, interfere
Intestinal Fortitude	N	Internal courage
Intimidate	V	Threaten
Intolerable	A	Not tolerable, cannot stand
Intolerance	N	Not tolerant, bearable
Intolerant	A	Not tolerable, able to stand
Intractable	A	Hard to control, manage
Intransigent	A	Without giving, compromising
Intrepid	A	Without fear. Bold
Intricate	A	Complex. Complicated
Intrigue	V	Mind-catching. Suspenseful
Intrinsic	A	Inherent, within
Introvert	V	Inward. Not open, outward
Introvert	N	Someone not open, outward
Intrude	V	Interfere
Intrusion	N	To intrude, interfere
Intrusive	A	Intruding, interfering
Intuitive	A	Insight. Intuition
Inundate	V	Cover completely. Overwhelm
Invalid	A	Not valid, fact, true, good
Invalidity	N	Not valid. Invalid
Invaluable	A	Value beyond calculation
Invariable	A	Not variable, changeable

Invective	A	Verbal attack, abuse
Inveigle	V	Lure. Entice
Invent	V	To create, devise
Invention	N	Invent. Create. Originate
Inventive	A	Able to invent, originate, create
Inventiveness	N	Ability to originate, invent
Inventor	N	One who originates new ideas
Invidious	A	Not fair, pleasant. Offensive
Invigorate	V	Refreshing, lively
Invincible	A	Not able to overcome
Involuntary	A	Not voluntary, by will, choice
Involved	A	Concerned. Into. Part of
Irate	A	Angry
Ire	N	Openly angry
Irk	V	Annoy. Pester
Irksome	A	To irk
Ironic	A	Say one thing, mean another in wit
Irradiate	V	Make clear by intellect
Irradicable	A	Unable to end, get out
Irrational	A	Not rational, normal
Irrationality	N	Without reason, rationale
Irredeemable	A	Not able to redeem, save
Irreformable	A	Not able to reform, change
Irrefutable	A	Unable to refute, disprove
Irregular	A	Not regular, customary
Irregularity	N	Being irregular
Irrelative	A	Not relative, pertinent
Irrelevant	A	Not relevant, pertinent

Irrepressible	A	Unable to hold, restrain
Irresolute	A	Not firm or sure
Irresponsible	A	Not responsible
Irresponsive	A	Not responsible, timely
Irritable	A	Able to irritate, agitate
Irritate	V	Spark resentment, hate
Isolated	A	Infrequent or once

-J-

Jabber	V	Talk on without coherence
Jack-of-all-trades	N	Do many things well
Jealous	A	Envious suspicion
Jest	N	Joke. Trick. Prank
Jester	N	One who jests. A joker
Jocose	A	Witty and humorous
Jocular	A	Jolly, jesting
Jolly	A	Open. Friendly, Cheerful
Josh	V	Joke, tease in jest
Journeyman	N	Experienced, knowledgeable
Jovial	A	Open, friendly natured
Joy	N	Happy, cheerful emotion
Joyful	A	Having happy, cheerful emotion
Jubilant	A	Extreme joy, high thrill
Judgment	N	To compare, judge, decide
Judicial	A	Prudent and careful

Judicious	A	Prudent, reasoned, wise
Juggle	V	Manipulate. Balance
Just	A	Reasonable. Fair. Right

-K-

Keen	A	Quick. Alert. Sharp
Keenness	N	A keen mental faculty
Keen-witted	A	Sharp, keen mental faculty
Keen-wittedness	N	Sharp, keen mental faculty
Keynote	N	A key or fundamental item
Kilter	N	On even keel. In order
Kind	A	Friendly, generous
Kindle	V	Ignite, start
Kindless	A	Not kind, friendly
Kindliness	N	Being kind, friendly
Kindly	A	Kind, friendly, sympathetic
Kingpin	N	Chief person in a group
Kindness	N	Showing or exhibiting kind deed
Kink	N	Unusual flaw or twist
Klutz	N	Someone awkward, clumsy
Knack	N	Unusual, ingenious ability
Know	V	Clear mental understanding
Know-how	N	Possessing knowledge
Knowing	A	Knowledge, knowledgeable
Know-it-all	N	Over confident of knowledge
Knowledge	N	Possessed wisdom, ability
Knowledgeable	A	Knowing. Learned

Knuckle down	V	Earnest effort
Knuckle under	V	Quit. Give in
Kudo	N	A "well done." Praise

-L-

Labor	N	Effort. Exertion. Work
Labor	V	To exert effort. Work
Laborious	A	Hard work, labor
Lack	V	Deficient, missing, short
Lack	N	Being deficient, missing, short
Lackadaisical	A	Slow. Without zest, zeal
Lackluster	A	Dull. Without life, energy
Laconic	A	Concise, offensive words
Lag	N/V	Behind. Slow
Landmark	N	First of its kind
Lapse	N/V	Come overdue, behind. Mistake
Large	A	Big. Many
Largehearted	A	Warm. Caring. Sympathetic
Large-minded	A	Open-minded. Knowledgeable
Last	A	End. Bottom. Lowest
Last-ditch	A	Final. Last
Lasting	A	Continuing on, enduring
Last minute	N	Final, ending move, action
Latitude	N	Free to act, do, choose
Laudable	A	Commendable. Noteworthy

Laudatory	A	To commend. Commendable
Launch	V	Go forth. Start
Laurel	N	In high standing, esteem, honor
Lavish	V	More than necessary
Lax	A	Not firm, resolute
Laxity	N	Being lax, not firm
Leading	A	Top. First
Learn	V	Obtain knowledge
Learned	A	Knowledgeable. To learn
Learning	N	Gaining knowledge
Least	A	Less. Lowest. Last
Legerity	N	Mental, physical agility
Legible	A	Understand writing
Legitimacy	N	Legal. Lawful
Legitimate	A	Legal. Lawful
Leisure	N	Idleness. Lax
Leniency	N/A	Not tough. Ease up. Easy
Less	A	Lower. Below. Decrease
Lessen	V	To be less. Decrease
Lethargic	A	Slow. Indifferent
Lethargy	N	Being slow. Indifferent
Lettered	A	Educated. Knowledgeable
Letter-perfect	A	Without error, flaw
Levelheaded	A	Reasonable in judgment
Level headedness	N	Even in temperament, rationale
Levity	N	Not constant. Changing
Liability	N	A disadvantage. Non-asset
Liable	A	Obligated. Responsible

Life blood	N	Crucial. Vital
Lifeless	A	Without life, vim, vigor
Life-style	N	Way of life
Light-headed	A	Not serious, sound
Lighthearted	A	Carefree. Happy. Joyous
Limelight	N	Center of attention
Limited	A	Restrained. Restricted
Limitless	A	Without limit. Continuous
Limp	V	Not stout, strong, steady
Limpid	A	Pure. Clear. Not complex
Literacy	N	Being literate, educated
Literal	A	Exact. Without error
Literary	A	Literate. Well read
Literate	A/N	Educated. Knowledgeable
Little	A	Small. Less than average
Liveliness	N	Active and energetic
Lively	A	Energetic. Alert
Lively Imagination	N	Keen, active intellect
Loath	A	Not willing. Reluctant
Loathe	V	Intense dislike. Hate
Loathing	N	An intense dislike
Loathsome	A	To be loath, detestable
Lofty	A	High above. Overbearing
Logic	N	Reasoned deduction. Rational
Logical	A	Skilled logic, systematic
Logical Thought	N	Rational, reasoning intellect

Loner	N	One avoiding others
Long-lived	A	Lasting. Enduring
Long-range	A	Ahead in time. Future
Look down	V	Belittle
Loquacious	A	Excessive talking
Loser	N	One unable to win, succeed
Lost	A	No longer possessed
Lower	V	Reduce. Make less
Low-grade	A	Below average. Inferior
Low-key	A	Low profile
Low-level	A	Low value. Below average
Low-minded	A	Low thoughts, behavior
Low-pressure	A	Little pressure, tension
Low-profile	A	Low visibility, attention
Low-spirited	A	Dejected, depressed
Loyal	A	Faithful. Dedicated
Loyalty	N	Being loyal, dedicated
Lucid	A	Clear knowledge
Lucidity	N	Clear understanding
Ludicrous	A	Foolish beyond belief
Lukewarm	A	Mediocre

-M-

Maladjusted	A	Not adjusted to society
Maladroit	A	No grace or skill
Malevolence	N	Grudging, ill will
Malevolent	A	Displaying grudging, ill will

Malice	N	Harmful intent
Malicious	A	Intending harm
Malinger	V	Shirk responsibility
Mammoth	A	Massive. Very large
Manage	V	Control. Direct
Management	N	Managing. Controlling
Manager	N	Someone who manages
Managerial	A	Management traits
Manipulate	V	Control actions, movements
Manipulation	N	Intelligent use, control
Manner	N	Behavior
Mannerism	N	Standard, expected behavior
Mannerless	A	Bad manners. Rude
Mannerly	A	Good manners. Polite
Mar	V	Scar. Fault
Marginal	A	Barely. Minimum
Marvelous	A	Almost above belief
Masterful	A	Most brilliant, skillful
Masterly	A	Display brilliance, skill
Mastermind	N	One who plans. Intelligent
Mastery	N	Control over. Expert
Matter-of-course	A	Natural events, course
Matter-of-fact	A	Of, to the facts
Mature	A	Developed. Grown full
Maturity	N	Being mature, developed
Maxim	N	A stated rule, fact
Maximize	V	Do to the maximum
Maximum	N	Most possible

Meager	A	Small. Little
Meander	N	Wander without cause
Meaningless	A	Without meaning, sense
Meddle	V	Pry uninvited
Mediate	V	Intermediary. Go between
Mediation	N	Serving to mediate
Mediocre	A	Barely satisfactory
Mediocrity	N	Being mediocre
Meditate	V	Mental pondering
Meek	A	Not strong. Weak
Menace	N	A threat
Mental	A	The mind or intellect
Mental Alertness	N	Quick, alert intelligence
Mental Capacity	N	Intellectual limit
Mental Deficiency	N	Lacking proper intellect
Mental Faculty	N	Intellectual ability, capacity
Mental Handicap	N	Intellectually restrained, confined
Mentality	N	Mental power
Mental Process	N	Intellectual functioning
Mental Void	N	Without knowledge, intellect
Mental Weakness	N	Lack of intellectual perseverance
Mentor	N	A knowing teacher
Merciful	A	Having mercy, compassion
Merciless	A	Without mercy, compassion
Mercy	N	Compassionate. Forgiving
Mere	A	The minimum. Only

Merit	N	Worthy of praise
Merry	A	Cheerful and lively
Methodical	A	By orderly procession
Meticulous	A	Exacting in detail
Might	N	Power. Strength
Mild	A	Even tempered disposition
Mindful	A	Pay heed. Attention
Mindless	A	Without knowledge, intelligence
Mingle	V	Mix
Minimize	V	Reduce. Decrease
Minimum	N	Least. Smallest
Minish	V	Diminish. Lower. Less
Minor	A	Less. Under
Minuscule	N	Extremely small
Minute	A	Extremely small
Misapply	V	Misuse. Misapplication
Misappropriate	V	Illegal use
Misbecome	V	Not becoming, fit, proper
Misbehave	V	Wrong behavior
Miscalculate	V	Judge badly
Mischievous	A	Minor tricks, pranks
Misconduct	V	Bad conduct
Misconstrue	V	Misunderstanding
Miserable	A	Bad. Substandard
Misfit	V	Not fit, adjusted
Misfortune	N	Bad fortune, luck
Misgiving	N	Doubt. Apprehension
Misguided	V	Led astray

Mishap	N	Unfortunate act
Misinterpret	V	Misunderstand
Misjudge	V	Bad, wrong judgment
Mislead	V	Lead astray, wrong
Mismanage	V	Manage badly
Mistake	V	Error
Mistaken	A	Be wrong, understand incorrectly
Misunderstanding	N	Incorrect understanding
Misuse	V	Use incorrectly, wrongly
Mix-up	N	Foul-up. Blunder
Moderate	A	Without excess. Reasonable
Moderation	N	Be moderate. Without excess
Modest	A	Not boastful, bragging
Modesty	N	Being modest
Monumental	A	Great. Tremendous
Moody	A	Uneven temperament
Moral	A	Discern right from wrong
Morale	N	Mental spirit
Moralist	N	Teach own morals
Moralistic	A	Concerned with rights & wrongs
Morality	N	Right and wrong principals
Moralize	V	Explain right from wrong
Motivate	V	Provide moving force
Motivation	N	Emotional drive to action
Motive	N	Reason. Driving force
Muddle	V	Mix up or confuse

Multitude	N	Many. Large amount
Mumble	V	Speak indistinctly
Mundane	A	Ordinary
Myriad	N	Infinitely large. Many
Mystique	N	Magical intrigue

-N-

Naïve	A	Gullible. Simple
Neat	A	In order. Tidy
Negate	V	Go or work against
Negative	A	No. Not positive
Neglect	V	Omit attention. Ignore
Neglectful	A	to neglect. Ignore
Negligence	N	Showing neglect by intent
Negligent	A	Fail to attend to
Negligible	A	Not of much importance
Nerveless	A	Without courage. Not bold
Nescient	A	Without adequate knowledge
Neutral	A	Not negative. Not positive
Nice	A	Friendly. Cordial
Nicety	N	Being, doing nice
Nimble	A	Mental agility, quick
Noble	A	High moral correctness
Nominal	A	Slight. Unimportant
Nonchalant	A	Not concerned, interested
Nonconformist	N	Not comply to norm
No-nonsense	A	Serious

Nonproductive	A	Not fruitful, productive
Nonsense	N	Not serious. Foolish
Normal	A	The norm, standard, average
Notable	A	Worthy of mention
Nought	N	Nothing. None
Nourish	V	Foster. Feed
Novice	N	A beginner. New person
Nuisance	N	Annoying
Null	A	No use of value
Nurture	N	Help grow, bring up

-O-

Obedient	A	Obeying. Complying
Obey	V	Comply. Follow direction
Oblige	V	Commit or compel for favor
Obliging	A	To favor. Give favor
Obnoxious	A	Crude. Rude
Obscure	A	Not clear. Hidden
Observant	A	Watchful attention
Obsession	N	Uncontrollable desire
Obsolete	A	Out of date
Obstacle	N	Something in way of objective
Obstinate	A	Overbearing. Stubborn
Obstruct	V	Hinder. Come between
Obtuse	A	Mentally slow to comprehend
Odd	A	Out of the usual. Strange

Oddity	N	Being odd, strange
Offend	V	Insult. Resent
Offensive	A	Disagreeable. Insulting
Omniscient	A	Limitless knowledge
One-track-mind	A	Handle only one subject at a time
One-upmanship	N	Skill of getting one up
One-way	A	Single direction, action
Open-eyed	A	Alert. Awake. Aware
Openhanded	A	Up front. Fair
Openhearted	A	Friendly, open personality
Oppose	V	Against
Opposition	N	Resisting. Opposing
Oppress	V	Restrain by harsh methods
Oppressive	A	Oppress with a force
Optimum	N	Ideal or best action
Oral	A	Speak. Speech
Orator	N	Skilled speaker
Orchestrate	V	Lead. Control
Ordeal	N	Trying, hard situation
Orderly	A	Tidy. In proper place
Ordinary	A	Routine. Normal. Common
Organize	V	Mesh together. Arrange
Orientate	V	Adjust. Become familiar
Original	A	New. Fresh
Originality	N	New. Creative. Original
Originate	A/V	Create. Bring into existence
Orthodox	A	Conventional. Normal
Orthodoxy	N	Be orthodox

Oscillate	V	Move, go back and forth
Ostracize	V	Expel. Cast out
Oust	V	Cast out. Expel
Outburst	N	Impulsive, offensive action
Outcast	A	Reject. Cast out
Outclass	V	Above in excellence
Outdo	V	Do better. Excel
Outgoing	A	Open, friendly manner
Outlandish	A	Foolish. Odd
Outlast	V	Last longer
Outlook	N	View of what is ahead
Outmatch	V	To do or be better
Out-of-date	A	Obsolete. Old
Outrage	N	Violent anger
Outrageous	A	Extremely violent action
Outshine	V	to outdo. Be superior
Outspoken	A	To freely spoken, disagree
Outstanding	A	Above all others. Preeminent
Outthink	V	Out wit. Out smart
Outwit	V	Outdo by sly, skill
Overbearing	A	Forceful. Arrogant
Overcome	V	Prevail despite obstacles
Overconfident	A	More confident than justified
Overdue	A	Past due. Late
Overextend	V	Extend beyond means
Overreact	V	React over requirement
Oversee	V	Watch over
Overshadow	V	Outdo. Outshine

Oversight	N	To miss. In error
Oversimplify	V	To omit pertinent facts
Overt	A	In the open. Not covered
Overwhelm	V	Overcome by force, weight

-P-

Pacify	V	To quiet, appease
Pall	V	Wear down. Boring
Palter	V	Squander without care, concern
Paltry	A	Little. Petty. Without value
Pamper	V	Treat too easily. Give in
Panic	N	Fear and loss of calmness
Paradox	N	Conflicting, true facts
Paragon	N	A model of excellence
Paramount	A	Primary or top importance
Paranoid	A	Unreal beliefs, fears
Paraphrase	N	Quote in part. Rephrase
Pare	V	Cut down. Reduce
Parity	N	Equal. Equality
Parlance	N	Language style
Parlous	A	Sly and risky
Parody	N	Bad double, imitation
Partial	A	Inclined toward. Favoring
Partiality	N	Be biased, inclined
Partisan	N	Extreme bias, preference
Passable	A	Just adequate

Passion	N	Strong seated emotion
Passionate	A	Strong or heated emotion
Passive	A	Inactive. Neutral
Passivism	N	Inactive, neutral
Passivity	N	Being inactive, neutral
Pathetic	A	Extremely sorrowful
Pathfinder	N	One who leads the way
Patience	N	Being reserved. Able to wait
Patient	A	Wait calmly
Patriot	N	One loyal to country
Patriotism	N	Feeling loyal to country
Patronize	V	Go along, lowering one's self
Paucity	N	Lack of. Little. Small
Peccant	A	Go against rule
Peculiar	A	Unique. Odd
Peculiarity	N	Being unique, odd
Pedant	N	One lacking in judgment
Peer	N	One of the same rank, equal
Peerless	A	Without peer, equal
Peevish	A	Immature. Bad humored
Pejorative	A	become negative, worse
Pell-mell	A/N	Confusing. Unorganized
Penetrate	V	To know, understand
Penetrating	A	Perceptive, discerning
Penetration	N	Sharp in mind
Penitent	A	Admit wrong. Regret
Pensive	A	Deep, sad in thought
Pep	N	Full of zest, zeal, spirit

Perceive	V	To recognize, know, understand
Perception	N	To be, make aware. Understand
Perceptive	A	To penetrate, know
Pendurable	A	Durable. Lasting
Perdue	V	Enduring. Lasting
Perfect	A	Without flaw. Exact
Perfectible	A	Able to make perfect
Perfection	N	Being perfect. Without flaw
Perfectionist	N	Reaching for perfection
Perform	V	To act or do. Accomplish
Performance	N	Performing. Accomplishing
Perfunctory	A	Casual. Indifferent
Permissive	A	Overly allowable, lenient
Perpetual	A	Go on and on. Lasting
Perpetuate	V	Cause to go on, continue
Perplex	V	Puzzle. Confuse
Perplexed	A	Being puzzled, confused
Perplexity	N	Being perplexed, confused
Persecute	V	Inflict ill will, trouble
Perseverance	N	Enduring, lasting will
Persevere	V	To endure, continue on
Persist	V	Continue on despite obstacles
Persistence	N	Being persistent, enduring
Persistent	A	Continue on despite obstacles
Personable	A	Friendly personality
Personality	N	Expressed individual attitudes

Personification	N	Embodiment of thing, idea
Personify	V	Serve as example
Perspicacious	A	Good perception, judgment
Perspicuous	A	Vivid, clear understanding
Persuade	V	Convince
Persuasion	N	Ability to convince
Persuasive	A	Be able to convince, persuade
Pert	A	Bold. Brash
Pertinacious	A	Stubborn. Persevere
Pertinacity	N	Being stubborn
Pertinent	A	Applicable. Relevant
Perturb	V	Upset. Alarm. Confuse
Pervade	V	Permeate. Penetrate. Prevail
Pessimism	N	Always think, expect worse
Pessimlstic	A	Expect worse. Not optimistic
Petty	A	Meaningless. Wirth little
Petulant	A	Insolent. Annoying
Pictured	V	Mental image, vision
Pillar	N	A mainstay
Pinnacle	N	At highest point possible
Pitfall	N	Shortcoming. Trap
Pitiless	A	Without pity, compassion
Pity	N	Sympathy. Sorrow
Placid	A	Under control. Calm
Platitude	N	Ordinary. Common. Trite
Plaudit	N	Praise. Approval
Plausible	A	Questionable
Pleasant	A	Pleasing. Agreeable

Pleasantry	N	Being pleasant
Pleasing	A	Agreeable. Pleasant
Pleasurable	A	Enjoyable. Gratifying
Pleasure	N	Good feeling. Pleasing
Pliable	A	Able to adjust, influence
Plod	V	Steady. Slow. Mundane
Poignant	A	Elicit compassion, emotion
Poise	N	Refined, dignified style
Polemic	A	Disrupt. Agitate. Incite
Polish	V	Social grace, refinement
Polished	A	Having social poise, grace
Polite	A	Courteous and considerate
Politic	A	Possessing prudent skill, wisdom
Polyglot	A	Conversant in language
Pomposity	N	Self-indulging or important
Pompous	A	Conceived self importance
Ponder	V	Think. Go over. Consider
Ponderable	A	Thinking. Going over. considering
Popular	A	Widely accepted, liked
Portentous	A	Pretense of self importance
Positive	A	In affirm, favor
Possessive	A	A desire to have, possess
Postulate	V	Speculate without proof
Postulator	N	One who postulates, assumes
Potency	N	Ability. Potential. Capacity
Potent	A	Powerful

Potential	A	Ability. Capacity
Power	N	Driving, moving force
Powerhouse	N	Mighty. Dynamic
Powerful	A	Mighty. Having great influence
Power of Mind	N	Ability to know, think
Power of Reason	N	Ability to use ration, reason
Power of Thought	N	Ability to think and originate
Practical	A	Sensible. Reasonable
Practical Knowledge	N	Realistic, useful mental capability
Practical Wisdom	N	Realistic, useful knowledge
Pragmatic	A	Speculate. Conjecture
Praise	V	Hold in high esteem. Commend
Precarious	A	Vulnerable. At risk
Precise	A	Exact
Precision	N	Being exact and finite
Predominant	A	Dominate without peer
Predominate	V	Dominate over, above others
Preeminent	A	Be, exist above others
Preferential	A	Prefer, choose over another
Prejudice	N	Judge before hand, facts
Prejudicial	A	Showing prejudice, favor
Premature	A	Before. Prior. Early
Premium	N	Extra, added value
Preoccupied	A	Mentally occupied
Prepare	V	To get, make ready
Preparedness	N	Being prepared
Preponderant	A	Over abundance
Preponderate	V	Dominant. Greater

Preposterous	A	Ridiculous. Outrageous
Potency	N	Very potent, powerful
Presence	N	One's bearing, being
Presence of Mind	A	Mental cleanness to act
Presentable	A	Acceptable to present
Prestige	N	Having renown, high stature
Prestigious	A	High honor, esteem, acclaim
Prevail	V	To win out, be on top
Prevailing	A	Existing above or superior
Prevalent	A	Dominant. Accepted
Pride	N	Esteem. Respect
Prime	A	Most important. First
Privilege	N	Special favor, consideration
Privileged	A	Having special consideration
Problem	N	Something requiring a solution
Problem	A	Hard to handle, deal with
Procrastinate	V	Put-off. Indecision
Prod	V	Push, stir to move
Prodigal	A	Overly generous, extravagant
Prodigy	N	One held in awe, amazement
Produce	V	to originate, bring forth
Productive Imagination	N	Creative results of the mind
Professional	N	One highly skilled
Professionalism	N	Exhibiting professional traits
Proficiency	N	Highly skilled
Proficient	A	Skilled, productive

Profound	A	Sound, innate mental power
Profound Knowledge	N	Broad intellectual depth
Progress	N	Improve. Advance. Forward
Progressive	A	Forward thinking
Proliferate	V	Multiply, increase rapidly
Prolific	A	Produce great many
Prominence	N	Being prominent
Prominent	A	Widely known, acknowledged
Promote	V	Foster. Further. Advance
Promoter	N	One who promotes, backs
Prompt	A	Quick. Timely
Promptitude	N	Being prompt, quick
Propagate	V	Spread. Emit
Propel	V	Push. Move
Propensity	N	Inclination
Proper	A	Correct. Right
Propitiate	V	Appease. Please
Propitious	A	Favorable
Propone	V	Put forth. Propose
Proponent	N	One who backs, promotes
Proposal	N	Submitting for view, review
Propriety	N	Proper and fit
Prosper	V	Flourish. Thrive
Prosperity	N	To prosper, succeed
Prosperous	A	Succeed. Flourish
Protégé	N	One trained by expert
Prototype	N	First of new breed, standard
Proud	A	Holding high esteem

Provident	A	Prudent. Wise
Provocative	A	Agitate. Stimulate. Provoke
Provoke	V	Stir up. Agitate. Excite
Provoking	A	To provoke
Prowess	N	Outstanding mental agility
Prude	N	One overbearing, crass
Prudence	N	Being careful, tentative
Prudent	A	Careful. Tentative
Prudential	A	Showing prudence, judgment
Prudish	A	Overly correct and proper
Pry	V	Unwanted inquiry, meddling
Prying	A	To pry
Punctilious	A	Excessive about detail
Punctual	A	Timely. One time
Pundit	N	Self-proclaimed expert
Pungent	A	Keen of mind
Pure	A	Without defect, impurity
Purge	V	Rid of unwanted parts
Purport	V	Suppose. Profess
Purpose	V	Intend. Reason
Purposeful	A	Having purpose, meaning
Purposeless	A	Without purpose, meaning
Puzzle	V	Perplex. Mix-up

-Q-

| Qualified | A | Capable. Able |
| Quality | N | A high state, degree |

Quantify	V	Determine by quantity, amount
Quell	V	To stop, silence, end
Query	N	Question
Quest	N	Venture. Seek. Pursue
Questionable	A	Uncertain. Doubtful
Quibble	N	Petty item, concern
Quick	A	Prompt. Fast. Ready
Quicken	V	To speed up, hasten
Quickness	N	Quick, perceptive mind
Quick-thinking	N/A	Quick in mental thought, action
Quick Wit	N	Mentally quick and alert
Quick-witted	A	Mentally quick and alert
Quip	N	Willy remark
Quirk	N	Unforeseen happening, twist
Quit	V	Stop. Cease
Quitter	N	One who quits too quickly
Quizzical	A	Unusually puzzling

-R-

Radiance	N	Shine with brightness
Radiant	A	Beaming, as goodwill, joy
Radiant	V	Emit warmth, goodwill
Rage	N	Violent anger
Rally	V	Renew, revive effort, action
Rampage	N	Violent action, behavior

Rare	A	Unusual. Not ordinary, common
Rarity	N	Being rare, uncommon
Rational	A	Sound, logical reasoning
Rationale	N	Rational reasoning
Rationalism	N	Use of reason
Rationality	N	Being rational. Able to reason
Rationalize	V	Interpret actions, reasons
Rational Faculty	N	Reasoning, rational mind
Ready	A	Prepared. Capable
Ready-made	A	Ordinary. Not original
Ready Wit	N	Mentally quick, alert, skillful
Realism	N	Being real vice idealistic
Realist	N	Practical reality, not idealistic
Realistic	A	Of reality, practical
Reality	N	Being real, fact
Realization	N	To realize
Reason	N	Rational thought
Reasonable	A	Within reason, justifiable
Reasoning	N	Rational deduction
Reasoning Facility	N	Logical, reasonable mental ability
Reasonless	A	Without reason, logic
Rebellious	A	Defiant. Opposing
Rebuff	N	Refute. Brisk refusal
Rebut	V	Formal refute, opposition
Recall	N	Memory. Memory ability
Receptive	A	Able, willing to learn
Rectify	V	Fix. Correct
Redress	N/V	To right a wrong

Redundant	A	In excess. Too much
Re-examine	V	Review again
Reevaluate	V	To rethink, reconsider
Refine	V	To make better, more pure
Refined	A	Cultured. Learned
Reform	V	Change for better. Correct
Refrain	V	To hold, keep back
Refreshing	A	New and invigorating
Refusal	N	Not accepting
Refuse	V	Turn down
Refute	V	Prove wrong, false
Regenerate	A	Renew. New vigor
Regress	N	Fall back. Lose ground
Regression	N	Regress. Move backward
Regret	V	Remorse. Sorrow
Regretful	A	to regret, feel sorry
Rehabilitate	V	Renew. Put back
Rehash	V	Go over again
Reject	V	Turn down
Rejuvenate	V	Give new, fresh life
Relapse	V	Fall back, slip back, to before
Relent	V	To give in
Relentless	A	Not giving in, relenting
Reliable	A	Dependable. Trustworthy
Reliance	N	Rely. Depend. Trust
Reliant	A	Trustworthy

Relinquish	V	Give up
Reluctance	N	Being reluctant
Reluctant	A	Not fully willing
Remarkable	A	Unusually good deed, feat
Remedial	A	to remedy, fix
Remedy	N	Fix. Correct
Remiss	A	Negligent. At fault
Remorse	N	Self sense of guilt
Remorseful	A	Felling remorse
Remorseless	A	Without remorse, guilt
Renascent	A	Renewed stamina, vim
Renew	V	Make new, over
Renitent	A	To resist, oppose
Renounce	V	Refuse. Rebut. Disown
Renovate	V	To fix up, renew, revive
Renown	N	High reputation
Renowned	A	Having high renown, reputation
Renunciation	N	To forgo, give up
Reorganize	V	Organize over, again
Repercussion	N	Reaction to action
Repertoire	N	Possessed special skills
Reprehend	V	Offend. Criticize
Reprehensible	A	Very offensive, criticizing
Repress	V	Suppress. Hold down, back
Repression	N	Being repressed
Reprimand	N	Official rebuke
Reproach	V	Blame for fault
Reproach	N	To blame for fault

Reprobate	V	Condemn. Disapprove
Reprobate	A	Without moral principles
Repudiate	V	Refuse. Deny
Repugnance	N	Utter dislike
Repugnant	A	Not agreeable
Repulse	V	Repel. Reject
Repulsion	N	Repel. Dislike
Repulsive	A	Repel. Dislike
Reputable	A	Good reputation
Reputation	N	Earned public character, stature
Repute	V	Supposed. Assumed
Requisite	A	Requirement
Resent	V	Bad feeling. Dislike
Resentful	A	To resent. Have bad feeling
Resentment	N	Bad, offensive feeling
Reserve	V	To hold back. Keep
Reserve	N	Something held back
Reserved	A	Held back, restrained manner
Reservoir	N	Place used for storage
Resilience	N	Ability to bounce back, recover
Resilient	A	Bounce back. Recover
Resist	V	Oppose. Go against
Resistance	N	To resist, oppose
Resistant	A/N	To resist, oppose
Resistless	A	Without resistance, opposition
Resolute	A	Firm. Determined

Resolution	N	Firm in resolve
Resolve	N/V	Firm determination. Decided
Resounding	A	Complete. Unqualified
Resource	N	Possessed ability. Resourceful
Resourceful	A	Possessing resource, ability
Respect	N/V	State of high esteem, regard
Respectable	A	Be held in high esteem, regard
Respectful	A	Being in respect
Responsibility	N	Being held accountable
Responsible	A	Accountable
Responsive	A	Ability to respond, answer
Restrain	V	Hold back
Restraint	N	Something that restrains
Resurge	V	Come or surge back
Resurgent	A	Rise or surge back, again
Retard	V	Hinder. Slow down
Retentive	A	To retain, remember
Retentivity	N	Capacity to retain, remember
Rethink	V	Think over again
Retribution	N	Due, just reward, punishment
Revive	V	Bring back to life
Rhetoric	N	Double talk with skill over words
Rhetorical	A	Using rhetoric
Rhetorician	N	One skilled in rhetoric
Rich Imagination	N	Unending mental originality
Ridicule	N	To belittle by joke
Ridiculous	A	Foolish. Outlandish
Righteous	A	Be, act right, proper

Rigid	A	Stiff. Firm. Not flexible
Rigidity	V	Be rigid
Rigor	N	Hard. Severe. Arduous
Rigorous	A	Hard. Strict. Severe
Rival	N	Opponent. Competitor
Rivalry	N	Standing rival. Competition
Robust	A	Strong. Healthy. Hardy
Rookie	N	A newcomer. Inexperienced
Rosy	A	Promising. Bright
Rough	A	Harsh. Not refined
Rouse	V	Agitate. Stir up
Rude	A	Bad in manner
Rudiment	N	Not yet fully developed
Rudimentary	A	New. Elementary
Run-down	A	Poor condition. Exhausted
Rusty	A	Not as capable/able as before
Ruthless	A	Without consideration, compassion

-S-

Sacrifice	N	Give up or go without something
Sagacious	A	Great judgment, mental ability
Sage	A	Wise and judicious
Sage	N	Someone wise and judicious
Salient	A	Main or major aspect
Sane	A	Rational mental faculty

Sanity	N	In control of mental facilities
Sapid	A	Pleasant. Interesting
Sapient	A	Wise. Knowing
Sarcasm	N	Remark in bad taste. Ridicule
Sarcastic	A	Displaying sarcasm
Satisfaction	N	Being satisfied, content
Satisfactory	A	Good. Adequate
Saucy	A	Not in good taste
Savior-faire	N	Verbal with and tact
Savvy	V	Know-how. Knowledge
Scant	A	Not sufficient, satisfactory
Scanty	A	Not sufficient. Meager
Scapegoat	N	One taking blame for another
Scarce	A	Rare. Uncommon
Scheme	N	A plan, plot
Scholar	N	Someone of knowledge
Scholarly	A	Having knowledge. Learned
Scoff	N	Contemptible
Scorn	N/V	Ridicule. Contempt
Scornful	A	Displaying scorn
Scruple	N	Indecision of right and wrong
Scrupulous	A	Proper, truthful, and careful
Scrutable	A	Questionable understanding
Scrutinize	V	Review closely, carefully
Scrutiny	N	Close, careful attention
Seasoned Understanding	N	Knowledge acquired overtime
Secluded	A	Hidden. Out of view
Second-guess	V	Question after the fact

Self-assertion	N	Assert one's self. Be insistent
Self-assurance	N	Confident in one's self
Self-centered	A	Overly concerned with one's self
Self-composed	A	Having composure, calmness
Self-conceit	N	Too high opinion of one's self
Self-confidence	N	Confident in one's self
Self-conscious	A	Overly concerned about one's self
Self-control	N	Having control of one's self
Self-defeating	A	Something that opposes itself
Self-determination	N	Providing one's own will
Self-discipline	N	Control of one's own actions
Self-doubt	N	Not confident in one's self
Self-esteem	N	Pride on one's self
Self-examination	N	Study one's own actions
Self-image	N	How someone views self
Self-important	A	Feeling overly important
Self-improvement	N	Individual effort to improve
Self-indulgence	N	Indulge on own desires
Self-interest	N	Concerned with one's own interests
Selfish	A	Not share, concerned with others
Selfless	A	Not selfish. Concerned with others
Self-made	A	Made or done by one's self
Self-opinionated	A	Conceited. Hold to own opinions
Self-reliance	N	Rely on one's self
Self-respect	N	Respecting one's self, values
Self-restraint	N	Control over one's self

Self-righteous	A	Showing self as morally better
Self-sacrifice	N	Sacrifice for others
Self-serving	A	Serve one's own interests
Self-starter	N	Supply own initiative
Self-sufficient	A	Without outside help, assistance
Self-taught	A	Learning by one's self, efforts
Self-will	N	Possessed with will to do, go forth
Semiskilled	A	Partially skilled
Senile	A	Mental decline due to age
Senility	N	Mental decline due to aging
Senseless	A	Without proper sense, meaning
Sensibility	N	Mentally receptive, rational
Sensible	A	Good sense of judgment
Sensitive	A	Compassion for others
Sensitivity	N	Being sensitive
Sentiment	N	Opinion formed in part by emotion
Sentimental	A	Acting from feeling
Serious	A	Important. Critical
Severe	A	Strict. Stern
Severity	N	Being severe
Shabby	A	Not appealing. Disgraceful
Shaky	A	Not steady, firm, dependable
Shallow	A	Superficial. Without depth, meaning
Shallowness	N	Without depth, substance
Sham	N	A deception
Shameful	A	Disgraceful
Shameless	A	Without shame. Not with modesty
Sharp	A	Keen, clear

Sharpness	N	Mentally quick and keen
Sharp-tongued	A	Harsh spoken
Sharp-witted	A	Quick, keen intellect
Sharp Wittedness	N	Quick, keen mind or wit
Shiftless	A	Unsteady ability, character
Shifty	A	Unstable character
Shipshape	A	Neat and orderly
Shirk	V	Evade. Get around
Shoddy	N	Bad quality. Inferior
Shortcoming	N	Fault. Not to expectation
Shortfall	N	Being, falling short
Shortsighted	A	Not looking, thinking ahead
Shortsightedness	N	Not thinking, planning ahead
Short-spoken	A	Speak briefly, to the point
Short-tempered	A	Lose temper easily
Shrewd	A	Clever. Cunning
Shrewdness	N	Keenly knowledgeable, clever
Shy	A	Quiet, reserved
Significance	N	Of some importance
Significant	A	Of importance
Silver-tongued	A	Convincing talker
Simple	A	Not complicated
Simple-minded	A	Mentally deficient, lacking
Simplicity	N	Not complicated. Simple
Simplistic	A	Simplify difficult problem
Sincere	A	Honest. Straightforward

Sincerity	N	Being sincere
Single-handed	A	Without assistance, help
Skeptical	A	Not convinced, sure
Skepticism	N	Being skeptic
Skill	N	Proficiency
Skilled	A	Having skill
Skillful	A	Having skill
Skirmish	N	Brief conflict
Slacken	V	Back-off. Do, become less
Slacker	N	One who lets up, slows down
Slipshod	A	Careless
Sloppy	A	Careless. Bad quality
Slopwork	N	Careless work
Sloven	N	One careless in manner, dress
Slovenly	A	careless in manner, dress
Slow	A	Not quick
Sly	A	Skillful, clever or devious
Small	A	Little
Small-minded	A	Not open. Narrow
Small-scale	A	Not big. Limited in scale, scope
Smart	A	Intelligent. Sharp
Smartness	N	Intellectually sharp, capable
Smooth-spoken	A	Smooth, polished in speech
Smooth-tongued	A	Smooth, eloquent in speech
Smug	A	Complacent. Self-assured
Snappy	A	Lively. Active
Snide	A	Sly and cruel
Snuffy	A	Stuffy. Not agreeable

Sociable	A	Friendly. Gregarious
Social	A	Friendly. Gregarious
Socialize	V	Be social with others
Soft-headed	A	Not smart, wise
Softhearted	A	Kindly. Not firm, strict
Solace	N	To console, comfort. Kind
Solicitude	N	Care. Overly caring
Solid	A	Stout. Firm
Solidify	V	Make solid, firm
Solitary	A	Alone
Solitude	N	Being alone
Somber	A	Drab. Dull. Boring
Sophisticated	A	Wise, polished or advanced
Sorrow	N	Grief. Regret
Sorrowful	A	With, of sorrow
Soundness	N	Valid in thought, reasoning
Sound Understanding	N	Thorough thought or knowledge
Sparing	A	Not in excess
Spark	V/N	Initiate. Stir. Stimulate
Sparkle	V	Actively clever, friendly
Sparse	A	Little. Thin. Shallow
Spartan	N	One with high discipline, bravery
Spearhead	N/V	Leading or moving force
Specialist	N	Expert n a skill, field
Specialize	V	Develop special skill in area
Specialty	N	A particular field of endeavor

Spectacle	N	Thing demanding visual attention
Speculate	V	Think of options. Ponder
Speculation	N	To speculate, guess
Speculative	A	Not sure, certain. Guess
Speedy	A	Quick. Prompt
Spirit	N/V	Enthusiasm. Drive. Cheer on
Spirited	A	Active. Lively
Spiritless	A	Without spirit. Lifeless
Spite	N	Of ill will
Spiteful	A	Vindictive. Hateful
Splendid	A	High worth, value. Great
Spontaneous	A	On impulse
Sporadic	A	Not regular, consistent
Spotless	A	Without flaw or fault
Spotty	A	Not consistent, regular
Spurious	A	False. Not real, true
Spurn	V	Contempt. Reject
Spurt	V	Short burst of activity
Squabble	V	Quarrel. Argument
Squander	V	Waste. Waste away
Stability	N	Stable. Firm
Stabilize	V	Make stable
Stable	A	Unmoving. Fixed. Firm
Staggering	A	Too great, many to imagine
Stagnant	A	Not moving. Inactive
Stagnate	V	Become stagnant
Stalwart	A/N	Strong. Unyielding. Firm
Stamina	N	Endure for long periods

Standard-bearer	N	One carrying a standard
Standout	N	Something superior as to stand out
Star	N	Someone who excels or shines
Staunch	A	Firm. Unrelenting
Steadfast	A	Firm. Resolute. Not wavering
Steady	A	Fixed. Constant. Controlled
Stealth	N	Undercover. Secretive
Stealthy	A	To be stealth
Stellar	A	Star, outstanding performance
Sterling	A	Of highest quality
Stimulant	A	To stimulate, increase activity
Stimulate	V	Ignite, arouse, or spur action
Stimulator	N	One who excites increased activity
Stimulus	N	Something that excites action
Stodgy	A	Mundane. Standard. Routine
Stoke	V	To fuel, stir up
Straight Thinking	N	Single direction of thought
Strength	N	Strong. Powerful
Strengthen	V	Become stronger, more powerful
Strenuous	A	Demanding great action, energy
Strict	A	Firm. Solid. Exact
Stringent	A	Being strict
Strive	V	Try. Attempt
Strong	A	Strength. Powerful
Strong-minded	A	Determination. Unrelenting will
Strong-willed	A	Determined. Headstrong

Studious	A	Study. Pay attention. Watchful
Stupefy	V	To stun, numb, dull
Stupendous	A	Overpowering. Overwhelming
Stupid	A	Not having normal intelligence
Stupidity	N	Being stupid, unknowing
Stupor	N	Mental dullness. Inattention
Style	N	Fashion or manner of something
Stymie	N	To interfere, obstruct, get in way
Stymied	V	To stymie, interfere
Suave	A	Sophisticated. Poised. Polished
Submissive	A	To submit, yield, give way
Subnormal	A	Below normal, average
Substandard	A	Below standard, expectation
Substantial	A	Great amount. Much. Many
Subtle	A	Not direct or mentally sharp
Succeed	V	Complete. Accomplish. Attain
Success	N	Complete correctly, favorably
Successful	A	Do with success
Succinct	A	Brief, concise & correct in speech
Succumb	V	Submit, yield, give in
Suffer	V	Realize pain, unpleasantness
Sufficient	A	Adequate. Enough
Suitable	A	Acceptable. To suit
Sullen	A	Quiet bitterness
Superb	A	Top quality. Without equal
Supercilious	A	Contemptible. Arrogance
Superficial	A	On the surface only. Shallow
Superficiality	N	Not meaningful, profound

Superfine	A	Super good, fine. Top quality
Superfluous	A	Excess. Not needed
Superior	A	Better. Greater. Top
Superlative	A/N	Superior. Better
Supporter	N	One who supports, backs, enforces
Supportive	A	To support, back
Suppress	V	Hold down or back. Stop
Supremacy	N	Be supreme, superior, above
Supreme	A	Best. Highest
Surly	A	Crass. Crusty. Rude
Surpass	V	Go past, beyond. Be superior
Surpassing	A	To surpass, go beyond. Excelling
Survive	V	To continue, carry on
Survivor	N	One who comes through repetitively
Sway	V	Waiver, give way. Charge
Swift	A	Fast. Quick. Prompt
Swiftness	N	Fast. Quick
Symbolize	V	To represent. Be a symbol
Sympathetic	A	Understanding. Express sympathy
Sympathize	V	To share in sympathy
Sympathy	N	Mutual feeling. Be understanding
Systematic	A	By system or methodical process

-T-

Tacit	A	Quiet. Silent. Without words
Taciturn	A	Tending to be quiet, not talkative

287

Tact	N	Diplomacy skill. Not offending
Tactful	A	Using tact, diplomacy
Tactless	A	Having no tact. Not diplomatic
Talent	N	Ability. Skill. Power
Talented	A	Possessing great abilities
Talkative	A	Talk too much, to extreme
Tangible	A	Being able to touch. Definite
Taskmaster	N	One who is demanding, exacting
Teach	V	Impart knowledge
Technique	N	A particular learned skill
Tedious	A	Tiresome, grueling, boring
Tedium	N	Be tedious, tiresome
Temerity	N	Too bold, reckless
Temperament	N	One's disposition or mood
Temperamental	A	Having excitable, erratic temper
Temperance	N	Restrained, reserved, even temper
Temperate	A	Restrained. Even tempered
Tempting	A	Inclined to entice, provoke
Tenacious	A	Firm. Very cohesive. Together
Tenacity	N	Firm. Resolute. Cohesive
Tender	A	Considerate. Gentle
Tenderhearted	A	Sympathetic at heart
Tension	N	Strain. Stress
Tenuous	A	Thin. Tiny. Little
Tepid	A	Not friendly, feeling
Terrific	A	Great. Super. Outstanding
Terse	A	Eloquent, concise, to the point
Thankful	A	Gratitude. Grateful

Thankless	A	Without thanks, gratitude
Thick	A	Slow to comprehend, learn
Think	V	Conceive by mental process
Thinkable	A	Conceive. Mentally possible
Thinker	N	One who thinks, plans
Thinking	A	Mental thought, action
Think-up	V	Mentally organize, devise
Thought	N	Conceived mental act, process
Thoughtful	A	Showing care, consideration
Thoughtless	A	Without thought or consideration
Thrift	N	Careful use of resource
Thriftless	A	Without thrift
Thrifty	A	To be thrift. Not wasteful
Thrive	V	Prosper. Flourish. Grow
Thwart	V	To intervene, obstruct, spoil
Tidy	A	Neat. Orderly
Timid	A	Shy. Afraid
Timorous	A	Timid. Shy. Afraid
Tiresome	A	Boring. Restless. Being tired
Tolerable	A	To tolerate, allow, bear
Tolerant	A	To bear with, tolerate, allow
Tolerate	V	Allow. Bear. Permit
Tough	A	Firm
Tough-minded	A	Tough, strong, firm of mind
Tradition	N	Time honored custom
Traditional	A	Being in tradition

Traditionalism	N	Being in tradition, custom
Traditionalist	N	One upholding tradition
Tranquil	A	At ease, calm
Tranquility	N	Be tranquil, calm, at ease
Transform	V	Change to something else
Transgress	V	Go beyond established limit
Travesty	N	Bad imitation, replacement
Treadmill	N	Boring. Repetitive. Monotonous
Tremendous	A	Great. Huge. Large
Trenchant	A	Clear cut. Keen
Tricky	A	Deceitful. Clever
Trifling	A	Superficial. Shallow
Trite	A	No longer valid, fresh. Stale. Old
Trivia	N	Unimportant in nature
Trivial	A	Of little value, worth
Troublemaker	N	One who routinely makes trouble
Trouble-shooter	N	One who looks for trouble to fix
Troublesome	A	Making, causing trouble
Truant	N	One who fails to work. Perform
Trustful	A	To trust, believe
Trusting	A	To trust, believe
Trustworthy	A	Be able to trust. Reliable
Truthful	A	Being at truth. Honest
Turbulent	A	Violent, disorderly
Turmoil	N	Confusion. Not stable
Typical	A	Serving as example of kind, type
Typify	V	Be typical

Ultimate	A	Conclusion. End
Unaccomplished	A	Not accomplished, skilled
Unacquainted	A	Not learned, taught, knowing
Unadvised	A	Done without forethought. Hasty
Unapt	A	Not apt, likely, skilled, able
Unassuming	A	Not forward, aggressive
Unaware	A	Not aware, knowing
Unbeatable	A	Unable to beat, conquer
Unbending	A	Firm. Resolute
Unbiased	A	Not biased, prejudiced
Unbounded	A	Without bounds or limits
Uncanny	A	Unreal, unnatural act or feat
Uncertain	A	Not certain, sure, positive
Uncertainty	N	Not certain, sure
Uncharitable	A	Without charity. Not forgiving
Uncomfortable	A	Not comfortable, agreeable
Uncommon	A	Not common, ordinary. Rare
Uncompromising	A	Not giving, relenting. Fixed. Firm
Unconventional	A	Not ordinary or standard
Unconversant	A	Lacking knowledge
Undaunted	A	Not failing, faltering
Undecided	A	Unsure. Not decisive
Undeniable	A	Unable to deny. Without question
Underhanded	A	Not open, above board, honest
Undermine	V	To weaken, wear away
Understand	V	To know, comprehend

Understanding	N	To understand
Understudy	N	One who studies under another
Undiscerning	A	Not good judgment, understanding
Undistinguished	A	Not looked up to, held in esteem
Uneasy	A	Not comfortable. Anxious
Unequivocal	A	Clear. Plain
Unerring	A	Without error, fault
Unerudite	A	Unlearned. Unskilled
Unexceptional	A	Plan. Common. Ordinary
Unfailing	A	Not fail. Reliable
Unfair	A	Not fair, just, equitable
Unfamiliar	A	Not known, recognized
Unfavorable	A	Not favorable. Against. Adverse
Unfeeling	A	Without feeling
Unfit	A	Not fit, able, capable
Unflappable	A	Composed. Calm
Unfortunate	A	Bad luck
Unfriendly	A	Not friendly
Ungracious	A	Not polite, pleasant
Unimaginative	A	No mental vision, inventiveness
Uninformative	A	Without knowledge, information
Uninformed	A	Not knowing, knowledgeable
Uninhibited	A	Without mental reservation
Unintelligent	A	Lack of intelligence
Uninteresting	A	Dull. Boring
Unique	A	Unusual. One of a kind. Rare

Uniqueness	N	Being unique
Unknowing	A/N	Not known. No Knowledge
Unknown	A	Not known, knowing
Unlawful	A	Not within the law. Not legal
Unlearned	A	Not learned, educated
Unlettered	A	Uneducated
Unlimited	A	Without bounds or limits
Unmannerly	A	Bad manners. Rude
Unmerciful	A	Without mercy, pity
Unmistakable	A	Without mistake, error, flaw
Unnerve	V	Lose nerve, confidence
Unorganized	A	Not organized, in order
Unparalleled	A	Without peer, match, equal
Unperceptive	A	Not knowing, discerning
Unperceptiveness	N	Not keen, penetrating, knowing
Unpleasant	A	Not pleasant, agreeable
Unpopular	A	Not popular, liked
Unprincipled	A	Without moral values
Unprofessional	A	Not professional, proper, correct
Unquestionable	A	Without question
Unrealistic	A	Not realistic, practical
Unreason	N	No reason, rationale
Unreasonable	A	Not reasonable, feasible, rational
Unreasoning	A	Without rational reason
Unrefined	A	Lack of culture, social bearing
Unrelenting	A	Not relenting, yielding. Fixed
Unrivaled	A	Without rival, match, equal
Unruly	A	Unable to control, manage

Unscholarly	A	Without knowledge, learning
Unscrupulous	A	Without principles, morals
Unseasoned	A	Not mature, experienced
Unselfish	A	Giving. Caring. Generous
Unsettled	A	Not settled, stable
Unskilled	A	Without skill, ability
Unskillful	A	Without skill, ability
Unsociable	A	Not sociable, friendly
Unstable	A	Not stable, firm, resolute
Unstoppable	A	Not able to stop, cease
Unsuccessful	A	Without success
Unsuitable	A	Not appropriate, compatible
Untaught	A	Without learning, education
Untidy	A	Not tidy, neat, orderly
Untrue	A	Not true. False
Untruth	N	Non-truth. False
Untruthful	A	Be untrue, false
Untutored	A	Unlearned. Uneducated
Unversed	A	Not learned, knowledgeable
Unwilling	A	Not willing. Reluctant
Unwise	A	Not wise, prudent
Unwittingness	N	Without wit. Dull
Unworthy	A	Not worthy, deserving, fit
Unyielding	A	Not giving, yielding
Up-and-coming	A	New. Promising
Upright	A	Just. Honest

| Useful | A | Of use, benefit |
| Useless | A | of no use, benefit |

-V-

| Vacuous | A | Without intelligence, thought |
| Vain | A | Empty. Futile |

| Valuable | A | Be important, meaningful, of value |
| Valueless | A | Without value or worth |

| Vast | A | Great. Huge. Immense |
| Veracious | A | Truth. Honesty |

| Veracity | N | Truthful. Honest |
| Verbalism | N | Word without form, meaning |

| Verbalist | N | Skilled orator, wordsmith |
| Verbose | A | Too long, wordy |

| Versatile | A | Adaptable. Multi-dimensional |
| Versed | A | Experienced. Skilled |

| Verve | N | Exuberant. Energetic |
| Vex | V | Troubling. Irritating |

| Vigilant | A | Watchful |
| Vigor | N | Vim. Vitality. Strength |

| Vigorous | A | Lively. Sturdy. Full of energy |
| Vim | N | Vigor. Zest. Vitality |

| Vindictive | A | Revengeful. Not forgiving |
| Violate | V | To break, penetrate in violation |

| Violent | A | Physical force, rage |
| Virtue | N | Good moral value |

Virtuous	A	Having virtue, high morals
Vision	N/V	Foresight. See into the future
Visualization	N	Foresee by mental picture
Visualize	V	Mental picture or image
Vitality	N	Vim. Vigor. Energy
Vitalization	N	Lively. Vim. Vigor
Vitiate	V	Go wrong, faulty, weak
Vivacious	A	Lively, with spirit, vigor
Vivid	A	Clear in vision, picture, thought
Vivid Imagination	N	Active, lively mind
Vocabulary	N	Word capacity, ability
Voluble	A	Talkative
Voluntary	A	Give freely. Free of will

-W-

Wade	V	To plunge into
Wander	V	Stray about without reason
Wane	V	Become less. Diminish
Wangle	V	Trick. Deceive
Wanting	A	Lacking. Deficient
Wanton	A	Without discipline, control
Warm	A	Affectionate
Warmhearted	A	Affectionate. Caring. Giving
Washed-up	A	No longer of benefit, use
Waste	N	Ruin. Spoil
Wasted	A	Ruined. Spoiled
Wasteful	A	To waste

Watchful	A	Observant
Weak	A	Not strong, steady
Weaken	V	Make weak. Lose strength
Weakhearted	A	Without conviction, courage
Weak-minded	A	Lack will power, judgment
Weakness	N	Being weak
Weariful	A	Tired. Weary
Weariless	A	Does not weaken, tire
Wearisome	A	Being weary, tired
Wear Out	V	Use up. Expend. Exhaust
Weary	A	Drained of strength, energy
Weighty	A	Important. Meaningful
Well-advised	A	Use wisdom, prudence
Well-bred	A	Well raised. Dignified. Sociable
Well-conditioned	A	Being well adjusted socially
Well-defined	A	Clear, distinct
Well-disposed	A	Good disposition
Well-done	A	Done correctly, properly
Well-founded	A	Based on solid reason
Well-groomed	A	Neat. Orderly. Tidy
Well-grounded	A	Well based knowledge
Well-handed	A	Well managed, controlled
Well-informed	A	Possessing great knowledge
Well-intentioned	A	Intending, meaning well or good
Well-known	A	Widely known
Well-meaning	A	Good meaning, intention

Well-off	A	In good condition
Well-read	A	Well informed. Knowledgeable
Well-rounded	A	Well developed, educated
Well-spoken	A	Speak with skill
Well-taken	N	To be well, happy, content
Well-timed	A	Timed to opportunity
Well-versed	A	Hiving expert knowledge
Whimsical	A	Erratic, unpredictable
Whiz	N	A wizard, genius
Wholehearted	A	Sincere and complete support
Wholesome	A	Healthy mind, morals, spirit
Wide-ranging	A	Wide in range, scope, context
Widely-read	A	Knowledgeable in many subjects
Wile	N	Deceive. Trick
Willful	A	With one's own free will
Willing	A	With free will. Without reluctance
Will-less	A	Without will
Wilt	V	Fade. Grow dim, weak
Willy	A	Skillful. Crafty
Winner	N	One who wins, comes out on top
Wisdom	N	Knowledge. Wise
Wise	A	Wisdom. Knowledge. Experienced
Wiseness	N	Of good judgment, wisdom
Wishful	A	Based on hope
Wishy-washy	A	Not firm, effective, steady
Wit	N	Power of mind, reasoning
Wits	N	Possess keen mental faculties
Withstand	V	Hold up. Oppose

Witless	A	Without wit
Witted	A	Having wit
Witticism	N	Sharp, penetrating joke
Witty	A	Having ample wit
Wonderwork	N	Successful, skillful undertaking
Wondrous	A	Held in wonder, high esteem
Wording	N	Convey in words
Wordplay	N	Skillful play at words
Wordsmith	N	One skillful at words
Wordy	A	Too many words
Workable	A	Capable. Able
Workaholic	N	One filled with capacity for work
Workhorse	N	One doing majority of the work
Workmanship	N	Quality of product
Work Over	V	Redo. To do again, over
Workup	N	Study. Preparation
Worldly-wise	A	Wise to the way of things
Worse	A	Less desirable or favorable
Worsen	V	To do worse
Worst	A	Most faulty, bad
Worthful	A	Of value, worth
Worthless	A	Without worth, value
Worthwhile	A	Worth time, effort
Worthy	A	Having merit, value worth
Would-be	A	Having potential, ability
Wretch	N	One dissatisfied. Bad disposition

Wretched	A	Totally disagreeable personality
Wrong	A	Erroneous. False. Amiss
Wrongdoer	N	One who does wrong
Wrongdoing	N	To do wrong
Wrongful	A	Being wrong
Wroth	A	Irate. Angry
Wry	A	Grim humor

-Y-

Yardstick	N	A standard, reference level
Yes-man	N	One always in agreement
Youthful	A	Young, fresh, refreshing

-Z-

Zeal	N	Spirit. Vigor. Enthusiasm
Zealot	N	One with zeal
Zealotory	N	Overfilled with zeal
Zealous	A	Having zeal
Zenith	N	Top. Uppermost point
Zest	N	Vigor. Enthusiasm
Zestfulness	N	Stimulating. Invigorating. Active
Zesty	A	Having zest
Zip	V	Swift, speedy. Invigorating
Zippy	A	Having zip, zest